"Vicki Carpel Miller and Ellie Izzo's book o ... c
side-effects of being a professional helper fi ... is
much needed book on vicarious trauma provi ... it
only an explanation for the unacknowledged ... e
work we do, but with concrete tools to addre.. ....g ....R,
helpers can both define the impact of "second - hand trauma" on their emotional health
as well as learn coping skills to manage it. This is a 'must read' for every serious therapist
who cares about his or her own emotional well-being."

Nancy J. Ross, LCSW, BCD
Co-founder of Collaborative Divorce and co-author of
"Divorce: A Problem to be Solved, Not a Battle to be Fought"

"Ellie Izzo and Vicki Carpel Miller have written what I am sure is a groundbreaking
survival guide for those who are constantly helping others – from medical professionals
to police and firefighters. The authors deserve praise for the valuable information they
provide, in a most articulate and interesting manner."

Randy Gengarelly, International Speaker, Consultant, and Trainer

"In ten years of working as a judge I have heard numerous stories, many of them quite
sad, some of them even horrible. As a professional you just deal with them. You do not
involve feelings and you try to resolve everything according to the law. The amount of
work makes you tired and sometimes hopeless because new cases are appearing every
day and the work seems endless. This book made me think that perhaps it is not only the
amount of work but also the content of this work that affects us. Until I read the book I
never thought that those stories stayed with me, even unconsciously. For me it was simply
the stress of work. DAY AFTER DAY THE PRICE YOU PAY: Managing Your Second -
Hand Shock™ helped me to understand that even the helper needs help himself and that
constant giving can empty you."

Mateja Dobovsek
Judge at District Court of Ljubljana
Slovenia, European Union.

"Betty Friedan, a feminist, in her book The Feminine Mystique (1963) coined the term
'The problem that has no name' to identify the full-time homemaker role which she
deemed to be stifling. Ellie and Vicki have now identified in their book DAY AFTER DAY
THE PRICE YOU PAY: Managing Your Second - Hand Shock™ another problem that has
no name: Helpers frequently find themselves compromised physically, emotionally and
spiritually without recognizing that they are suffering from Vicarious Trauma. Finally,
they have identified a valuable topic for all helping professionals that has not previously
been addressed."

Dr. Rosalyn Golfman
PhD, Certified Psychologist

"Practitioners in many professional arenas experience Secondary Traumatic Stress and Vicarious Traumatization as a result of constant exposure to traumatic client problems and due to their empathy for their clients. It is essential that care providers learn to recognize and respond to these issues with both professional support and a self-care regime. DAY AFTER DAY THE PRICE YOU PAY: Managing Your Second - Hand Shock™ is an engaging and substantive contribution to the field. It engages the reader in self-reflection of one's own work, provides insightful case examples and offers a novel guide to help mitigate the impact of STS. It will be embraced by those eager to help themselves so that they can continue to help others."

Mary L. Pulido, Ph.D.
Executive Director
The New York Society for the Prevention of Cruelty to Children

"Vicarious trauma is one of the most important issues for any professional working with traumatized and/or difficult clients. And all indicators are that this problem is increasing. From legal to healthcare professionals, from therapists to collaborative divorce advisors, and many others, there is a growing need for information like this excellent book for keeping yourself balanced and healthy while being exposed to the increasing stresses in our high conflict and high stress society."

William ("Bill") Eddy, LCSW, Esq.
Co-Founder & President, High Conflict Institute, Scottsdale Arizona
Author, Attorney, Therapist, Speaker

"This is the first book that I am aware of which addresses the issues of secondary trauma on those of us who are working with victims of trauma. Ellie Izzo and Vicki Carpel-Miller have taken their many years of experience and created a way for the rest of us to understand and appreciate the hidden costs, psychological, emotional, physical and personal, to professionals who have dedicated themselves to helping families. The examples given in the book ring true to life; we will all recognize these stories. The scientific information about brain function is the most up-to-date research about what is really going on. The authors write in a clear, straightforward style so that this book will be read and used by their colleagues for many years to come; we will do a better job for our clients having read DAY AFTER DAY THE PRICE YOU PAY: Managing Your Second - Hand Shock™."

Rita S. Pollak
Past-President, International Academy of Collaborative Professionals

DAY AFTER DAY
THE PRICE YOU PAY:
Managing Your Second - Hand Shock™

DAY AFTER DAY THE PRICE YOU PAY:
Managing Your Second - Hand Shock™

Dr. Ellie Izzo, PhD, LPC, and,
Vicki Carpel Miller, BSN, MS, LMFT

This publication is designed to provide accurate and authoritative information about the subject matters covered. It is sold with the understanding that the publisher is not rendering legal, mental health, or other professional services in this book. If expert assistance, legal services or counseling is needed, the services of a competent professional should be sought.

Names and information identifying private individuals have been changed to preserve anonymity. Many quotations have been modified to protect confidentiality and to demonstrate the principles of the book. Some examples are slight alterations of real cases, while other examples were inspired by real cases but are completely fictional. Quotes and news publications are accurate and names are real.

Izzo, Ellie, 1953-
Carpel Miller, Vicki, 1952-
DAY AFTER DAY THE PRICE YOU PAY: Managing Your Second - Hand Shock™ / by Ellie Izzo and Vicki Carpel Miller
Includes bibliographical references.
ISBN 978-0-9815090-0-6

First printing: May 2008

Editor: Danielle LeClair Rakoz
Book design: Pierpoint-Martin
Printing: Lightning Source Inc.

Publisher:
Published by Janis Publications USA Inc.
www.janispublications.com

Printed in the United States of America

DAY AFTER DAY
THE PRICE YOU PAY:

Managing Your Second - Hand Shock™

By Ellie Izzo, PhD, LPC
and
Vicki Carpel Miller, BSN, MS, LMFT

This book is dedicated
to all of our clients:
past, present, and future.

TABLE OF CONTENTS

ABOUT THE AUTHORS

Dr. Ellie Izzo, LPC, PhD

Dr. Ellie Izzo is co-founder of Vicarious Trauma Institute in Scottsdale, Arizona. She is a Licensed Professional Counselor and has been in clinical practice since 1982. She received her Master's Degree from Long Island University in 1982 and her Ph.D. in Health and Human Service from Columbia Commonwealth University in 2007.

Ellie created and developed the Rapid Advance Process, a standardized five-session brief model of counseling, in response to a serious problem experienced by millions of professionals in the human service field – Vicarious Trauma.

She authored a book on Rapid Advance Psychotherapy entitled The Bridge to I Am: Rapid Advance Psychotherapy. Dr. Izzo presented Rapid Advance Psychotherapy to the American Counseling Association convention in Atlanta in 1997 and again in Honolulu in 2008.

She presents for numerous conferences and conventions, hosted a call-in radio show in Phoenix and served as Self-Help Editor for a nationally syndicated trade magazine. She is currently the psychology advisor for AZ Teen Magazine and runs several ongoing groups called the Encouragers, where people meet to offer each other peace, support and acceptance.

She also serves as a Divorce Coach, Child Specialist and/or Team Manager in the process of Collaborative Divorce, whereby a team of professionals help a couple move through divorce respectfully, without litigating.

Vicki Carpel Miller, BSN, MS, LMFT

Vicki Carpel Miller, BSN, MS, LMFT, is co-founder of Vicarious Trauma Institute in Scottsdale, Arizona. She received a Bachelor of Science degree in Nursing from the University of Minnesota in 1970 and in 1989 she received a Master's degree in Counseling Psychology from Nova University in Fort Lauderdale, Florida.

As a Registered Nurse and Licensed Marriage and Family Therapist in private practice for over 18 years, she specializes in the treatment of Vicarious Trauma, divorce-related issues and blended families.

Vicki is an internationally recognized presenter and trainer in the field of Collaborative Practice, training family lawyers, licensed mental health and financial professionals world-wide in the Collaborative Divorce Full Interdisciplinary Team Model of Collaborative Practice with Collaborative Divorce Team Trainings.

She is co-founder of the Collaborative Divorce Professionals of Arizona and functions as a Divorce Coach, Child Specialist and/or Team Manager in Collaborative Divorce files. Vicki has received advanced training in family mediation, narrative mediation, interest-based negotiation, Collaborative Law and Collaborative Divorce Interdisciplinary Team Practice.

Based on their success with the Rapid Advance Process created by Dr. Izzo in her book The Bridge To I Am: Rapid Advance Psychotherapy, Vicki and Ellie launched the Vicarious Trauma Institute and went on to co-author this book, DAY AFTER DAY THE PRICE YOU PAY: Managing Your Second - Hand Shock™ to extend healing to all in the helping professions. They provide training and consultations to organizations, groups and individuals around the world on the subject of Vicarious Trauma.

Ellie and Vicki's website is www.VicariousTrauma.com.

They can be contacted at 480-991-4119 or by email at:
    Ellie Izzo   info@vicarioustrauma.com
    Vicki Carpel Miller   info@vicarioustrauma.com

ACKNOWLEDGMENTS

We believe it is an honor and a privilege to acknowledge the dedication of the people in the helping professions. It is our professional responsibility to talk about and approach this sensitive subject with courage and forthrightness, in the hope that others will follow. We want to offer help to the helpers.

We are grateful to those who have come before us and whose work we have found invaluable in writing this book. The pioneering work of Pearlman, Saakvitne, Figley, Begley, Carl, Joseph, Weingarten, MacIan, and Wilson has provided a strong foundation of research about this subject. It is likely we have left out some important contributors. Failure to acknowledge or cite these important works at any point in the book was simply an oversight. We apologize and ask your forgiveness.

We thank all who have contributed their stories to this book. For their protection and the safety of their clients, names, place, and details have been changed.

Most importantly, we acknowledge our families and our friends who have suffered the effects of Vicarious Trauma with us and have supported us in our healing and in the writing of this book. Your understanding, patience, compassion, and love have been and remain life-sustaining.

Ellie and Vicki

INTRODUCTION

We estimate that there are over 100,000,000 helping professionals worldwide. That is a staggering number. Hard work and dedication can take a heavy toll on the helper. The cost of helping others cannot really be assessed by the naked eye. Perhaps that is why so little has been written or done about it. In truth, the toll for many helpers is high, and the amount of recovery resources is low.

Even though you are well-trained and complete continuing education on a regular basis, we fear you remain unconscious and uneducated about the signs and symptoms associated with Vicarious Trauma. Intrusive imagery, cynicism, poor memory, isolation, volatile moods, irrational fears, lack of spiritedness, physical problems or symptoms are noticed but ultimately disregarded or attributed to other better-known diagnoses. How many times have you heard people ask, "How do you do this all day, every day?" If you think about it, it really is not strange. Listening to trauma stories all day, every day, takes a heavy toll on your emotional, mental, physical, and spiritual well-being.

We ourselves have frequently returned home in a negatively altered emotional and physiological state from a long week of helping others. We too have endured our share of sleepless nights, elevated anxieties, periods of depression, and physical ailments. We have heard our families and friends complain that we are impatient, distant, and estranged from them. We too have suffered. We are not ashamed to admit it. That is why we have written this book.

It is troubling to us that most ethical codes do not mention the welfare of the helping professional when discussing Vicarious Traumatization. We believe, and we hope you agree, that it is downright dangerous to continue to revere the image of dedicated, self-sacrificing workers who never care for their own needs. This view perpetuates the unvoiced epidemic of Vicarious Trauma. We believe it is severely underreported in our population. We trust there are a lot of us out there suffering in silence.

The welfare of the helping professional for him/herself is an ever-increasing issue of ethical importance. Professional boards advocate self-care. Self-care implies that the individual is responsible for preventing the problem when it does occur. Professional helpers often get blamed, in very shaming ways, for stress responses, rather than being encouraged to see stress as a natural response and as an opportunity for introspection and feedback. We truly believe our approach maintains and strengthens the clear and good judgment of the helping professional and, therefore, may well be the best way to serve the client, patient, or person.

Part One

Chapter One: A Serious Situation

Anna, a 40-year-old woman, came to counseling for hypnotherapy. Her presenting problem was that she had developed a fear of flying. She had flown often for her paralegal job of 17 years, which included traveling to different states and gathering information for depositions. The phobia had gotten so bad, even the thought of buying a ticket triggered a panic attack. Her law firm represented plaintiffs in medical malpractice and other wrongful death lawsuits. Some of these suits pertained to accidental deaths in airplane crashes. She developed her flying phobia just about the time she was gathering evidence in a wrongful death suit involving a small private jet.

Anna heard many traumatic stories and studied numerous vivid, disturbing pictures over the length of her career. She would write lengthy motions and memos that were filled with graphic details of death, severe illness, and mutilation. She described her role in the firm as the "empathy agent." She was always the first contact with whom clients would share their appalling story. Anna listened to the clients' narratives as if it were happening to her. She would share the clients' pain and demonstrate her compassion for them. She was also very good at her job and brought in huge settlements for clients and for the firm.

After further questioning, it was revealed that this married mother of two also suffered from depression, irritability, emotional numbness, and insomnia. She described herself as "robotic:" going to work every day and coming home every evening only to place herself in front of the TV to watch Crime Scene Investigation. She isolated herself from the outside world and barely interacted with her family. She reported that she had no tolerance for the day-to-day troubles of her growing children and often reacted to them with anger and impatience. Small issues were eliciting high levels of anxiety and she was becoming hypervigilant about not getting injured. Activities that were commonplace for her, such as driving, swimming, and shopping, all evoked a fear response. Anna started to sob as she mumbled that there was no happiness or meaning in her life anymore and the world was an awful place to be. Anna had a lot more to deal with than a flying phobia; she was suffering from Vicarious Traumatization.

Anna, Paralegal

What is Vicarious Trauma? The technical definition of Vicarious Trauma is a permanent transformation in the helper's inner experience resulting from empathic engagement with the client's traumatic material (Pearlman & Saakvitne, 1995). More simply put, Vicarious Trauma is a set of cognitive, emotional, physical, and spiritual disturbances that result from helping trauma survivors. Every time a helper interacts with a client, he or she is putting him or herself at risk. All of us are secondary witnesses to trauma nearly every day. All we need to do is watch television, listen to, or read the news. A traumatic response in any individual is the result of a number of processes, some of them biological, some of them psychological. It is also important to remember that any experience of trauma is in the "eye" of the beholder. There are cultural, historical, and childhood frames of reference that may help one person go into a trauma response while the situation will not affect another in quite the same way (International Trauma Consultants, 2006).

Vicarious Trauma is more than secondary trauma, which is defined as indirect exposure to trauma through a firsthand account or narrative of a traumatic event. Vicarious Trauma is a condition that anyone in a helping position can experience. It is characterized by a painful set of symptoms that result from utilizing controlled empathy while listening to or seeing traumatic narrative content (Wilson & Thomas, 2004).

Controlled empathy by itself is a vigorous neurological activity. When a helping person is listening to the shocking, sad, or awful stories of another, it may look like he or she is calmly sitting and listening. But the activity going on inside the listener's brain and body looks anything but calm. Not only is the helper absorbing the shocking story, he or she must respond to the content in a constrained manner that is geared to helping the suffering person. If you are or know someone in the helping professions, it is useful for you to understand the neuroscience of controlled empathy.

It is important to note that controlled empathy and automatic empathy are not the same. Neurologically, they travel in different circuitries in the brain (International Trauma Consultants, 2006). Because controlled empathy is automatic empathy interrupted, it casts a much greater strain on physiology, emotions, and spiritual well-being.

So what is automatic empathy? The neurological activity of automatic empathy involves a specific system of neurons called mirror neurons. The process forms a neurological loop originating from the mirror neurons in the pre-frontal cortices of the brain and traveling throughout different regions of the brain. This neurological loop creates in the listener a full body sensation *as if* the listener is actually experiencing the event. The neurons form a specific brain circuitry that underlies the empathic impulse and ultimately helps the listener adopt another's point of view. The circuitry sets the stage of the human imagination; it is a right brain activity and the helper imagines the event as if it were happening to him or her (Wilson & Thomas, 2004).

Researchers studied the empathic response by locating the neurons in the anterior cingulae of the brain that respond to a patient being poked with a needle. These neurons are referred to as sensory neurons. Remarkably, these researchers also found that some of these neurons fire with equal strength when the patient witnesses someone else being poked. When this type of sensory neuron is fired, changes take place throughout the body as if the witness is having the pain. New brain scan techniques have enabled scientists to prove that the ability to empathize is an intrinsic part of the brain. Empathy neurons dissolve the barrier between the self and the other (Kramer, 2007).

Empathy, the ability to share another's emotions, is rooted in infancy. For example, newborn babies will cry in response to the cries of another infant (Kramer 2007). Early in life we learn to imitate, matching emotions to expressions and events. We use that information to predict each other's emotions and act compassionately or vicariously, depending on the situation.

A pattern of the brain strain associated with controlled empathy is observed starting with the activation of the visual cortex. As the listener hears the revolting story he or she begins to visualize it in the mind, as if it is actually happening. The brain is struggling with another's upset. In this process, called controlled empathy, the helper has to rev up his or her internal resources to remain calm (International Trauma Consultants, 2006). This taxes the right hemisphere of the brain because the activated mirror neurons want to surge from it, but the helper has to hold back because he or she needs to remain controlled. Imagine yourself setting a top spinning and then needing to immediately interrupt its gyrations; it's like going against a force of nature.

An 8-year old girl was brought to therapy by her maternal grandparents. She had been experiencing ongoing night terrors for three months. Her father was incarcerated 3 years ago and her mother had passed away. This was the only information given to me at the time I made the appointment by telephone. I was curious to find out how this child was so dramatically abandoned by her parents. The grandmother insisted that she meet with me prior to my taking a session alone with the child.

Here is what she told me: When the little girl was 4 years old, her parents separated. "My daughter was a beautiful person, a model, and she had a beautiful heart. My son in law was an abuser, in disguise. No one believed that a man of his sophistication and stature in the community could be so evil and violent. My daughter asked for a divorce and in the beginning of that process we thought that he was going to cooperate. But his anger was only building and he was determined to take little Maya away from her mother. My daughter reported all of the minor incidents of domestic violence to the police, but none were deemed severe enough for the police to take action. One day, when Maya was at school, he intruded into my daughter's place of business, doused her with gasoline and lit her on fire." (At this point the grandmother was weeping and I had to repress my own natural gag reflex.) The grandmother continued to share that her daughter survived the attack for about 36 hours after the horrific incident. She said that her screams of agony from the burn unit were blood-curdling. After telling the police that it was her husband who perpetrated the act, her daughter died.

All I keep thinking about is that now Maya has no mother and a father who will never be released from prison. The grandmother has lost her only daughter. She wanted Maya to get help for the intense trauma she sustained. I am giving this help, but it is exacting a painful toll on my own well-being.
Dora, Psychotherapist

When a person engages in automatic empathy, rather than controlled empathy, he or she can let out the tension freely. This process has a preferable physiological impact on the brain. The right brain and left brain work together to resolve the process of automatic empathy. The brain activity of a person experiencing automatic empathy, a healthy neurological process, is much like the top spinning until it slows down and then stopping on its own. Once the left and right brain have achieved a calm balance, or homeostasis, the empathic person has the ability to respond to the story and more easily access higher mind dynamics for helping. These dynamics might include forgiveness, hope, faith, and courage. These spiritually-based dynamics are important to utilize in traumatic situations.

Empathy plays a critical role in many facets of life, from management and sales to friendship and parenting, and to the many dimensions of the helping professions. It leads the way to compassion, moral awareness, and spiritual well-being. When the complicated neurological activity of controlled empathy is coupled with the neurological strain of traumatic content, people are faced with the probability of suffering Vicarious Traumatization, or Second - Hand Shock.

Chapter Two: The Neuroscience of Trauma

The biological effects of Second - Hand Shock, or Vicarious Traumatization, fall into a range of trauma categories that researchers distinguish from each another, although there is not necessarily agreement about how to do this. The research in this area is still evolving and will continue to undergo many transitions. One thing that much of the research maintains is that the terms shock, stress response, trauma response, acute stress disorder, and acute or chronic post-traumatic stress disorder, burnout, and compassion fatigue all have stress in common. Stress is an alarm reaction to a stimulus the person appraises as emotionally charged or threatening. This state can range from exhilaration to mild or severe discomfort. Trauma is stress run amok. Understanding the movement from stress to trauma demands a basic understanding of the structure of the brain.

The brain is structured into three main parts:

1. The cortex, which includes the outer surface, where higher thinking and spiritual skills arise. This includes the frontal cortex, which is the most recently evolved portion.
2. The limbic system, which is the center of the brain where emotions evolve.
3. The brain stem, which contains the reptilian brain that controls basic survival functions (Healing Resources Info, 2005).

Stress originates in the amygdala, which is in the mid-brain and is also called the primitive brain. This is the dwelling place of the fight or flight reaction; it produces hyperarousal, which is a normal and necessary response to threat. The fight or flight reaction prepares the body for defensive acts through a cascade of sympathetic nervous system firings and the release of stress hormones, the most well known of which are epinephrine and adrenaline. Our physical reactions match the potential demands on us. Our pupils dilate so we can sense what is going on around us. Our skin conductivity intensifies so that the hair on our skin will stand up and we can sense vibration. The heart's output increases so that more blood is pumped to the extremities, readying our arms and legs to run if necessary. Our respiratory rate intensifies as more oxygen is provided for our tissues. At the same time, blood is diverted from the digestive system, producing the sensation of gnawing in the stomach. Once the perceived danger is past, the body halts the alarm reaction and restores the body to homeostasis, or a state of rest (Weingarten, 2003). Thus, the body ratchets up for defense and then must ratchet down for recovery.

Stress throws our nervous system out of whack, but only for a short period of time. Within a few days or weeks the nervous system calms down and we revert to a normal state of equilibrium. This return to normalcy is not the case when we are being traumatized. Trauma stress can be distinguished from routine stress by assessing the following:

1. How quickly the upset is triggered.
2. How frequently the upset is triggered.
3. How intensely threatening the source of the upset is.
4. How long the upset lasts.
5. How long it takes to calm down (Healing Resources Info, 2005).

If we feel frozen or, conversely, if we feel in a state of active emotional intensity, we are experiencing emotional trauma, even though we may not be consciously aware of the level of distress. Trauma actually changes the structure of the brain at the point where the frontal cortex, the emotional brain, and the survival brain converge. One significant finding is that the brain scans of people with relationship or developmental problems or learning and social problems related to emotional intelligence reveal similar structural and functional irregularities as individuals suffering from Post-Traumatic Stress Disorder (PTSD) (Healing Resources Info, 2005).

PTSD was originally categorized as a set of symptoms incurred as a result of experiencing traumatic or life-threatening events. Such events originally included:

- natural disasters,
- wartime events,
- horrific accidents or crimes, and
- experiencing or witnessing horrific injury or fatalities.

Other potential sources of trauma that are often overlooked include:

- falls or sports injuries;
- surgery, particularly emergency surgery;
- serious illness;
- birth trauma; and
- hearing about violence or the death of someone close.

In addition, traumatic stress that influences the brain is caused by:

- poor relationships with primary caregivers,
- forced separation very early in life, and
- chronic misattunement of caregiver to the child's attachment signals for reasons such as physical or mental illness, depression, or grief.

Recent research also suggests that early life trauma creates vulnerability and higher risk for experiencing future traumatic responses (Healing Resources Info, 2005). Research has revealed that emotional trauma can result from such common occurrences as:

- an auto accident,
- the breakup of a significant relationship,
- a disappointing or deeply humiliating experience, and
- the discovery of a life threatening illness, or a disabling condition.

Traumatizing events take a serious toll on those involved, even if the event does not cause physical damage. Emotional trauma contains three elements:

- it was unexpected,
- the person was unprepared, and
- there was nothing the person could directly do to prevent the event from happening (Healing Resources Info, 2005).

Remember, it is not the event itself that determines whether something is traumatic to an individual, but their perception of the experience. Also, remember that how a person will react to a particular event is not predictable. For someone who is used to being in control of emotions and events, it may be surprising, even embarrassing, to discover that something like job loss can be so debilitating.

Repetitive recall of traumatic memories and chronic intermittent hyperarousal are characteristic of post-traumatic stress. Hyperarousal and memory dysfunction implicate the limbic brain regions, including the amygdaloidal complex, hippocampal formation and limbic cortex, such as the orbit frontal and anterior cingulae areas (Liberzon et al., 1999). Many areas of the brain are activated and involved when you are experiencing a traumatic event.

The neuroscience of trauma can also be discussed by considering the structure in the brain stem called the locus coeruleus. It has many connections throughout the brain to activate and alert a person, even interrupting the individual if necessary to ensure that attention is paid to high-priority stimuli. When a person is repeatedly exposed to a threat or exposed to an extreme threat, the locus coeruleus actually changes; it becomes hyper-responsive to stress signals (Weingarten, 2003). This produces the felt experience of hypervigilance for the individual; in effect, the locus coeruleus itself suffers trauma or brain damage. The hyper-responsiveness of this part of the brain sets the primitive brain working in overdrive, while the higher brain functions less. The victim feels stressed and tense much of the time.

The limbic system also plays a key role in the body's response to trauma. The amygdala assigns emotional significance to incoming signals and the hippocampus evaluates, categorizes, and stores information. Coordination between both structures is paramount for normal functioning. One reacts to incoming information and the other makes sense of it. Under conditions of extreme stress, an agitated amygdala interferes with and could shut down the hippocampus, resulting in a number of symptoms that are associated with the long-term effects of trauma, such as memory loss and intrusive imagery.

Under extreme stress, the amygdala takes charge of the experience and expression of fear. It will forge conditions between the elements (e.g., heart rate, respiratory rate, blood pressure) in the threatening situation and a fear response without the individual having any awareness that it is even happening. Thus, a person may be left with a fear response to triggers in the environment that actually make no sense to her or him (Weingarten, 2003). Furthermore, neurons have a great deal of difficulty in forging connections to the higher mind, where forgiving, hopeful, and peaceful thinking are accessed.

The more the brain has to deal with, the more it will adapt and change. Eventually these adaptations can become maladaptive. People who have been repeatedly exposed to the most troubling kinds of interactions and events and who have worked diligently to meet these challenges may find that they respond with heightened reactivity so that they feel overwhelmed a great deal of the time. This sensitization creates mountains out of molehills so that small issues that would typically not bother others present major upsets for affected person. Children and adults who have been exposed to domestic abuse are a particularly vulnerable group in this area and have frequently been found to be suffering from PTSD (Healing Resources Info, 2005).

The relationship between traumatic emotional stress, hippocampus injury, memory loss, and traumatic amnesia was examined. This relationship is well-documented, and it has been demonstrated that animals and humans exposed to high levels of stress, fear, and arousal for prolonged periods commonly experience learning deficits and memory loss ranging from the minimal to the profound (Schore, 2003). As stress and arousal levels increase, learning and memory decrease in accordance with the classic U-shaped curve. These memory deficits are due to disturbances in hippocampus activation and arousal and in the corticosteroid secretion that can suppress neural activity associated with learning and memory, thereby inducing hippocampus atrophy. Trauma can induce disturbances in all aspects of spiritual, social, and emotional functioning and affect the growth and survival of dendrites, axons, synapses, interneurons and neurons, all of which are essential for healthy brain functioning (Joseph, 1999).

With the significant information presented above, it is evident and should be frightening to note that trauma, in whatever form, is a high-risk neurological event and can result in permanent damage to the brain and extremely painful consequences for the person.

Chapter Three: The Psychology of Trauma

T he mental health response to trauma has undergone enormous change in the last decade. Trauma psychology has become a field of study and treatment in and of itself. Acute Stress Disorder was not included until the Diagnostic and Statistical Manual of Mental Disorders IV was published. This only came about through those involved in crisis intervention repeatedly pointing out the need for a conceptual classification that addressed the traumatic event in first few weeks of stress and not just Post-Traumatic Stress Disorder after the first month. The classification also served the practical purpose of providing insurance coverage. The most current version of the DSM is the Fourth Edition, Text Revision (DSM-IV-TR, 2000). The DSM-V is not expected to appear until 2011 or later (Baldwin, 2007).

Linking acute stress and early interventions along a continuum that recognized the need for ongoing and long-term intervention for individuals who developed PTSD was the purpose of using trauma psychology as an umbrella term to describe this evolving specialty. Trauma psychology includes short-term crisis intervention, sometimes referred to as Critical Incident Stress Management (Carll, 2007).

In its original sense, trauma involves exposure to a life-threatening experience. This fits with its original, or phylogenetic, roots in life-or-death issues of survival, as pointed out in the previous chapter. Yet, people who have been exposed to violations by individuals or institutions they must depend on or trust also show symptoms similar to those caused by Post-Traumatic Stress Disorder, even if their abuse was not directly life-threatening (Lee, 2006).

Trauma experiences shake the foundations of our beliefs about safety and shatter our assumptions of trust. They can break the spirit of an individual and set that person up to forget the power of faith. Because these events are perceived so far outside of what we would expect, they provoke reactions that feel strange and crazy. Even though the reactions appear unusual and disturbing, they are actually characteristic and quite common. Trauma symptoms are probably adaptive and originally evolved to help us recognize and avoid dangerous situations quickly, before it is too late. Sometimes these symptoms resolve within a few days or weeks of a disturbing experience.

Not everyone who experiences a traumatic event will develop PTSD. We create meaning out of the context in which events occur. Consequently, there is always a strong subjective component in people's responses to traumatic events (Baldwin, 2007).

How is it that an event can cause an emotionally traumatic response in one person and not another? Let's take a closer look at this phenomenon. We already mentioned that trauma is in the eye of the beholder and that many factors affect an individual's particular experiencing of a traumatic event. Some of the factors involved are:

- the severity of the event;
- the individual's history, which may not even be recalled;
- the larger meaning the event represents for the individual, which may or may not be immediately evident;
- the coping skills, values, beliefs, and spiritual views held by the individual, some of which may have never been identified; and
- the reactions and support from family, friends and professionals (Baldwin, 2007).

PTSD is officially classified as an anxiety disorder, but some have argued that it fits more closely with the dissociative disorders. Others feel it belongs by itself. There has also been some discussion over differential diagnoses for simple versus chronic traumatic histories such as Complex PTSD or the proposed DESNOS diagnosis (Disorders of Extreme Stress, Not Otherwise Specified). Recent work suggested that DESNOS may be more frequent among individuals whose subsequent adult traumas complicate chronic or unresolved childhood traumatic experiences and that DESNOS has important implications for treatment (Baldwin, 2007). Classification issues such as these will probably continue through field trials for the DSM-V.

Common effects or conditions may occur following a traumatic event. Sometimes these responses can be delayed for months or even years after the event. Often people do not even initially associate their symptoms with the precipitating trauma. Symptoms are more likely to result from a commonplace trauma, such as surgery or a minor car accident, if there were earlier, overwhelming life experiences. This may result from state-dependent learning, in which previous responses to a terrifying event are repeated even though more appropriate responses could be used, such as proactive defenses that would enable parents to help their hurt child rather than freeze (Baldwin, 2007). These defenses fit into three categories: physical, emotional, and cognitive. The following chart is condensed from the writings of Jaffe, Segal, and Dumke (2005):

PHYSICAL	EMOTIONAL	COGNITIVE
Eating Disturbances	Depression, Despair	Memory Lapse
Sleep Disturbances	Anxiety, Panic Attacks	Difficulty Making Decisions
Sexual Dysfunction	Fearfulness	Decreased Ability to Concentrate
Low Energy	OCD Behaviors	Feeling Distracted
Chronic Unexplained Pain	Irritability, Anger Emotional Numbness	ADHD Symptoms

Additional symptoms can occur with a severe precipitating event and also as a delayed reaction. One set of symptoms is categorized as re-experiencing the trauma and includes:

- intrusive thoughts,
- flashbacks,
- nightmares, and
- sudden flood of emotion or images related to the event.

Another set of symptoms is categorized as emotional numbing and avoidance and includes:

- amnesia;
- avoidance of situations that resemble the initial event;
- detachment;
- guilt feelings;
- grief reaction;
- altered sense of time;
- increased arousal;
- hypervigilance, jumpiness, or extreme sense of being on guard;

- overreactions, including sudden unprovoked anger;
- general anxiety;
- obsessions with death; and
- insomnia (Jaffe et al., 2005).

When unrecognized, emotional trauma persists and remains unresolved and can create lasting difficulties in an individual's life. One way to determine whether an emotional or psychological trauma has occurred is to look at the recurring problems an individual is experiencing. These can serve as clues to an earlier situation that causes dysregulation in the structure or the function of the brain. Common personal and behavioral effects of emotional trauma include:

- substance abuse;
- compulsive behavior patterns;
- self-destructive and impulsive behavior;
- uncontrollable reactive thoughts;
- inability to make healthy professional or lifestyle choices;
- dissociation or splitting off parts of the self;
- feelings of ineffectiveness, shame, despair; and
- a loss of previously sustained beliefs and spiritual values.

Common effects of emotional trauma on interpersonal relationships include:

- inability to maintain close relationships,
- inability to choose appropriate friends or mates,
- sexual problems,
- hostility,
- recurring arguments with family members or colleagues,
- social withdrawal, and
- feeling constantly threatened (Healing Resources Info, 2005).

Trauma takes a huge toll on the individual and untreated, can destroy the life of its victim.

Chapter Four: When Is It Vicarious Trauma?

Anyone can be traumatized. The risk for Post-Traumatic Stress Disorder increases with exposure to trauma. Chronic or multiple traumatic experiences are likely to be more difficult to overcome than most single instances. PTSD is also more apt to occur if passive defenses such as freezing or dissociation are used rather than active defenses such as fight or flight. There is some evidence that early traumatic experiences, especially if prolonged or repeated, may markedly increase the risk of developing PTSD after traumatic exposure as an adult (Baldwin, 2007).

Our focus now turns to an additional aspect of Second - Hand traumatic exposure that includes both graphic and painful material and primarily affects workers who help trauma and disaster victims. This includes psychologists and other mental health professionals, lawyers, paralegals, judges, custody evaluators, EMTs, nurses, physicians, clergy, police, criminologists, dentists, journalists, fire and rescue workers, family members, and close friends. In fact, anyone who is exposed to an overdose of victim suffering is at risk for secondary traumatization. If you add the component of controlled empathy, which we discussed in Chapter 2, you've got Vicarious Trauma. Several studies of helping populations show that at least 53% of helping professionals describe themselves as survivors of some form of childhood trauma (Pearlman & Saakvitne, 1995). This historical situation increases the possibility of contracting Vicarious Trauma.

If you work with the stories of many trauma/disaster victims, be aware of the three major risk factors for Vicarious Trauma:

1. exposure to the stories or images of multiple trauma victims,
2. your controlled empathic sensitivity to their suffering, and
3. any unresolved emotional issues that relate affectively or symbolically to the suffering seen or heard.

Experts warn that symptoms of Vicarious Trauma should be taken seriously and steps should be taken to heal, just as you would take action to heal from a physical ailment. As with any physical condition, the amount of time or assistance needed to recover from emotional trauma varies from person to person.

Several job characteristics can fuel Vicarious Trauma:
1. cumulative impact of client trauma stories,
2. repetitive contact with troubled people,
3. intense personal contact with these people while you work with them,
4. ongoing involvement,
5. the ethical pressure of maintaining confidentiality, and
6. the giving role in general (Lee, 2007).

Untreated Vicarious Trauma can cause helping professionals severe debilitating anxiety that persists for months or perhaps years. It can truly break the spirit of the helper. Because these helpers are not directly involved in the event, their distress often goes undetected and untreated.

Let's go back to our introductory case study of Anna. Here is the story in her own words:

> You requested that I write about the case that affected me the most. Boy, to pick just one is tough. Numerous cases have affected my life in various ways. Tragic cases involving children are probably the toughest. Most cases I emotionally deal with by rationalizing that 'this could not happen to me or most people because....' One case that I will pick, however, is one that could happen to anyone.

> It involved a young mom in her 30's. She was a strong person who was a good wife and a good mom. She had a problem with alcohol when younger but was successfully in recovery. In 1998, she had a routine pap smear. It was done by a doctor in Arizona, but sent to a lab in New Mexico. It was read as normal. In 1999, she had another routine pap smear and it was sent to the same lab in New Mexico for interpreting. Again, it was read as normal. The young mom was having abnormal menstrual problems and pain. In 2001, a new pap smear revealed malignant cervical cancer. The 1998 and 1999 slides were misread. Both slides were read by the same lab technician, who was later fired. By the time the 2001 slide was read, it was too late for this young

mom. All radical treatments were fruitless. She would have had better than an 80% chance of recovery if the malignancy had been properly discovered in 1998 or 1999. She died about one year after the 2001 slide was read. She experienced horrible pain and suffering during this time. Pictures showed that she slowly dwindled away until she looked like a skeleton.

The pain and suffering her children felt was unbearable and unfair. They will not be able to have their mom around when they graduate high school, college, get married, or have children. It has been traumatizing for her husband, who loved her dearly. The kids have had many struggles since their mom died, especially the youngest child, who has been in and out of a lot of trouble.

The slides should have been read properly. The lab tech should have been better supervised by the lead pathologist. The lab techs in that facility should not have been under pressure to read over 50 slides a day. A better system should have been in place. This young mom should be alive today. This case was heartbreaking for me. I could literally feel her pain up until the last day of her life, including the sadness she felt for her children.
Anna, Paralegal

Anna was at risk for Vicarious Trauma because of her intense and ongoing professional involvement with the husband and children of the victim. Her professional involvement began to impose a personal bias because, from Anna's point of view, this was a traumatic event that could certainly have happened to her. Additionally, she had to control her empathic response, taxing her brain's ability to automatically resolve what would have been a grievous but normalizing and balanced response.

When we are deeply distressed or just can't shake a client's story, we are probably having difficulty negotiating the biochemical stress response or we may have become less and less effective at doing so. We may even be surprised at what might trigger the stress response from that story: an item in a magazine, an image we see out of the corner of our eye, a character in a story we are reading. We are struggling in our own ability to calm our sympathetic nervous system. Helping professionals will find their inner experience of self, others, and their Higher Power transformed in ways that parallel the experience of the trauma survivor. In other words, symptoms of Vicarious Trauma (VT) closely parallel symptoms of PTSD.

Here are some of the warning signs of VT:

- Emotional exhaustion: the emotional overextension of contact with others that drains your energy. Emotional exhaustion includes feelings of apathy, entrapment, dissatisfaction, hopelessness, helplessness, nervousness, irritability, discouragement, and emptiness.
- Depersonalization: an unfeeling and hardened response to others.
- Reduced personal accomplishment: a decreased a sense of professionalism or achievement in your work with others.
- Somatization: this includes changes in appetite, gastrointestinal disturbance, anger, low self-esteem, self-doubt, and impaired judgment and reasoning.

The symptoms of Vicarious Trauma run parallel to those of PTSD and include:

- distressing emotions;
- hyperarousal;
- disruptions in the cognitive schema of helper identity, memory, and belief system;
- intrusive imagery, such as nightmares or recurring visualizations;
- emotional numbing;
- inability to tolerate strong emotions or hypersensitivity to emotionally charged stimulations, such as movies or television;
- feeling fearful or overly concerned for family members;
- dissociation;
- somatization, in which psychological symptoms present as physical ailments and physical illness;
- isolation and diminished capacity to enjoy significant activities; and feelings of incompetence (Saakvitne & Pearlman, 1996).

Controlled empathy is the capacity to efficiently and accurately monitor another's state of being and it is the specific channel through which VT occurs. It is precisely in the empathic witnessing of the client's experience that helpers risk fundamentally and permanently having their world-view altered. Empathic capacity is the professional's aptitude for controlled empathy and it varies among helping professionals.

Overuse of controlled empathy can spawn an existential crisis called the Abyss. The Abyss is the intense emotional cauldron of a deregulated affective state expressed in altered patterns of attachment, relationship, experience of horror, abandonment by humanity, and spiritual challenge of meaning (International Trauma Consultants, 2006). A person in this state has little or no awareness or control over his/her emotions, internally or externally. Furthermore, the Abyss becomes profoundly disturbing to professionals who believe that their training renders them invulnerable to extreme emotional stress. The helper may not be conscious that anything is even happening or may go into a form of denial, based in shame that something like VT could happen at all.

Helping professionals frequently work with clients who have suffered PTSD. This type of client presents stories we hear routinely and these stories have an effect on us. In the performance of their duties, helping professionals may have any of four types of witnessing experiences. These experiences directly impact helpers and clients, but because of the central role helpers may play in clients' lives, the effects can also ripple outward. If helping professionals are not able to manage their witnessing experiences effectively, harmful consequences may extend to personal relationships, colleagues, and the community at large.

The following table is taken from an article in Counselor magazine (Weingarten, 2004): Common Shock: Witnessing Violence in Clients' Lives.

	AWARE	UNAWARE
EMPOWERED	Effective and Competent Position 1	Misguided, Possible Malpractice Position 2
DISEMPOWERED	Ineffectual And Stressed Position 3	Abandoning, Possible Malpractice Position 4

Allow us to explain. The first witnessing position is Stage One: empowered and aware. The helper is someone who feels effective and competent to address the situation at hand, who is not dissociating from or avoiding the trauma situation, who is hearing the story with controlled empathy and not finding herself or himself in an elicited trauma response. This is a win-win situation for all concerned. Following is a submission from a lawyer who was able to maintain a Stage One (empowered and aware) position with his client:

> I had a family retain my services for a medical malpractice case that hit really close to home. The mother of the family had a minor back problem for which she elected to have surgery. The surgery was successful and initially the mother seemed to be enjoying an uneventful recovery. On the third day after the surgery, one of her children came for a visit and noticed that her mother's color was ashen and upon feeling her mother's forehead, noticed that her mother was feverish. Her mother complained of a sharp pain on her lower left side. The child quickly reported this to the nursing staff and was assured the doctor would be in to check on her mother sometime that morning. The child left to go to work and assured her mother she would return later that day.
>
> When she returned, her mother's fever was further elevated, she was semiconscious and unable to communicate effectively. The child went back to the nurses' station and received a report that the doctor had seen the mother earlier in the day and had ordered antibiotics to be administered intravenously. Even though the daughter was very upset, she went home that evening, slept fitfully, and awoke early and returned to the hospital to be with her mother. When she got there, the bed was empty. Her mother had died in the course of the night and no one had called her or the family to let them know.
>
> I handled this case for the family, but it was very difficult for me. My own mother had died shortly after bypass surgery five years earlier. I had to keep my own history and personal pain out of the conference room and out of my negotiations. I actually consulted with the therapist that I worked with when my mother died to ensure that I remained objective and untouched by my own trauma response. I won, you know. They gave the woman the wrong antibiotic; she was septic and they missed it. The clients won a huge award, but, sadly, lost their mother.
> Martin, Lawyer

The Stage Two witnessing position, empowered and unaware, occurs when helpers respond as if they are aware but not checking in with the severity, significance, or impact of what the client's story is telling them. In this situations, helpers are not connecting with the actuality of the trauma content and how it relates to their client. This may be seen as abandonment and is also a form of malpractice. Helpers are responding as if they know what they are doing and will find themselves ineffective at best, guilty of passive behavior toward their client and of possible malpractice at worst. In reality, the helpers are not effectively treating their clients; they are minimizing the client story because of their own VT. Their personal symptom of VT is numbing out or dissociating from the trauma content narrative. This process has also been called Collusive Resistance, in which helpers unconsciously or consciously join their clients in avoiding a painful and traumatic experience (Fox & Carey, 1999). Following is a Stage Two story from a mediator:

A husband and wife were going through a divorce with my help. I am a lawyer/ mediator. On numerous occasions during our meetings, the wife attempted to describe to me, in the presence of her husband, detailed and graphic accounts of conflictual interactions between she and her husband, and between her husband and their two small children. She described verbally violent episodes that she perceived as very traumatizing to herself and her children. She related intimidating, demeaning, and threatening conversations that the husband vehemently denied. The husband alleged that the wife was exaggerating and that she was simply trying to discredit him to me. Her rationale, he explained, was to increase her parenting time and cause him to have additional child support to pay. There were never any police reports filed, and I had no other collateral information to support the wife's narratives. The wife eventually stopped relating her stories and agreed to move forward with the mediation.

In my assessment of the situation, the husband presented as calm, rational, logical, and cooperative. The husband never had a bad word to say about the wife; in fact, he spoke very highly of her parenting skills and her relationship with the children. He denied any and all allegations presented by the wife, citing his children's desire to spend time with him as their Little League coach and active participant in their lives. Divorcing is a very stressful situation, and although at times I saw impatience on the part of the father, I assumed it was appropriate behavior based on the stress level of the couple going through this divorce. My role was to facilitate a negotiated agreement, a win-win solution for this couple, and so we proceeded with mediation and reached agreement over the course of several meetings.

One day, after the final agreement had been reached, the husband contacted me by cell phone to discuss changing a certain phrase in the parenting agreement. Once our conversation had concluded, the husband thought the phone call was disconnected. However, he failed to disconnect from the call and I overheard his communications with the children while he continued driving with them in the car. These communications were demeaning, threatening, abusive, and violent, containing accusations and name-calling about the mother. The children were crying and begging him to stop. I was horrified that I had so misjudged the situation.

At this point, the agreement was finished and no further meetings were scheduled, with the exception of having the clients come in to sign the document. I believed my job was done. The following week, the couple came to sign the documents at my office. Once finished, the wife left first, while the husband used the rest room, or so I thought. She got into the elevator, he jammed his hand between the elevator doors before they closed, and forced his way in. He stabbed her once in the chest and several times in other parts of her body. She died later at our local hospital.
Fred, Lawyer/Mediator

There was nothing lacking in Fred professionally. He was trained well but had become numbed due to Vicarious Trauma. Because of his unrecognized VT he failed to intervene on behalf of his female client. Unfortunately, after years of hearing similar stories, Fred had become desensitized or numbed when hearing narratives regarding domestic abuse. His lack of awareness precipitated poor professional judgment and ultimately cost the life of one of his clients. Now Fred has to deal with the ongoing grief of thinking about two children who have lost both their parents to something much worse than divorce. To this day, Fred worries about the professional and civil repercussions of this case and his future cases.

Stage Three witnessing is found when professionals are highly conscious of what needs to be done and are aware of the situation, but feel powerless to provide any viable help. This is the most traumatizing witness position for helpers to face. Helpers who are keenly aware of the client's situation but feel helpless to do anything about it will be of little or no use to their clients and highly stressed by their work. This situation places helpers in the role of little more than a bystander. The following heart-wrenching story was told by a hospital-based social worker:

> I work at a children's hospital with transplant cases. Most of the time, people die before we can get them the organs they so desperately need. One case that plays over and over in my mind is a case of a 7-year-old boy who had been waiting for 3 months for a kidney. His health was declining fast. He was brought in shortly before Christmas in a physiological crisis. Dialysis was no longer effective and his system was crashing. His doctor was concerned that he would not survive the weekend. For 48 hours I lived on the telephone in my office. I called every hospital, every ER, every social service agency, every transplant team, desperate to find a warm body to talk to. I so wanted to save this little boy's life. With each voicemail I left and each menu I had to navigate, I felt more and more desperate. I didn't want to have to tell his parents I failed. But I did, and he died.
>
> Never before in my job had I operated in a scenario where I was so powerless. For months, I felt directly responsible for his death. After a year of therapy, I am finally coming to terms with the failure of our medical system. I no longer blame myself, but I sure am bitter.
> Grace, Licensed Clinical Social Worker

Grace suffered with the most distressing of the witness positions. Helping professionals are frequently haunted by events in which they were extremely conscious of what needed to be done but felt powerless or lacking in any form of support to provide it.

In a Stage Four witnessing position, unaware and disempowered, helping professionals are passive in relationship to the urgent needs of their clients and ultimately abandon clients because of this ignorance and lack of awareness. The professionals' own Vicarious Trauma has overridden both their professional skills and personal awareness so that the helpers are physically present but emotionally and professionally absent. The following is an account of a Stage Three story provided by a psychologist:

I am a trauma survivor myself and have worked for over 20 years with survivors of sexual abuse in my practice. As a child, my parents crossed sexual boundaries with me but not with malicious intent. I had done forgiveness work with my therapist several years before this case walked through my door and I believed that I had healed from my own personal trauma. The client shared with me a history that was brimming with many levels of domestic violence. Her father, an alcoholic and drug addict, terrorized and assaulted every member of her family. When the client was 3 years old, she remembered her father fondling her genitals as he gave her a bath. This sexual abuse intensified over time so that by age 8, he was forcing her older brother to perform anal intercourse on her while her father masturbated.

When I heard the story, I mistakenly assessed that the client would overcome this heinous form of abuse as I had survived mine. Wrong! The client carried far more disturbance than I tuned into in the course of our work together. While I utilized certain therapeutic techniques that were appropriate for this type of client, it certainly was not enough for someone who presented with this type of childhood trauma. In retrospect, the client needed to be under the ongoing care of a psychiatrist for medication evaluation, she needed to seek out and become a member of an adult survivor of childhood sexual abuse support group, and she needed to be treated by a more experienced therapist who specialized in this type of sexual violence.

Eventually the client's symptoms became worse and she developed hallucinations and paranoia. I referred her for a more intensive program of treatment. I probably needed to do that after our first consultation, but I really thought I had my finger on the pulse of her problem. I think about her often and wish I had acted sooner. While I don't think I did the patient any direct harm, I don't believe I did her much good.
Bethany, Psychologist

Bethany had to take a close look at how Vicarious Trauma had desensitized her response to sexual assault clients and how her own treatment and her belief about other people's treatment impacted her assessment skills in this case. She believed that if she could survive her childhood trauma and function at a high level, so could anyone else. Her judgment was impaired, her ability to assess the needs of her client was impaired, and her treatment lacked the dimension that the client deserved to receive. The phenomenon of countertransference, which played a significant role in this case, will be examined more closely in Chapter 5.

Vicarious Trauma may cause permanent changes in the helper's world-view. The world begins to be perceived as a dark place where no one is emotionally safe. The pathway to the spiritual perspective is broken. Helping professionals may suffer compromised basic needs. Safety, trust, esteem, intimacy, and control needs are adversely affected in those affected by Vicarious Trauma (Saakvitne & Pearlman, 1996).

One such extreme example is George, a pastor of a large congregation in the southern United States:

> I serve a large congregation in the deep South. I am revered and thought of as a man of kindness, great wisdom, and vision. Congregants approach me on a daily basis for advice, wisdom, forgiveness, and hope for the future. I rarely have a day that I am not bombarded with needy people. The classic line I hear is, "Pastor George, can I just have a moment of your time?" Even when I attend social events, someone needs to unload on me. When I first took on this congregation, I encouraged my congregants to reach out for my help; sometimes you have to be careful what you pray for!
>
> Over the years, I found myself in a deepening spiritual crisis. It is really hard to preach the word of God when you are in conflict about whether He's really listening. I am so depressed about the person I have become. When I was a student in seminary, I was so faithful about the protection offered in a relation with God. Today I am not the same person. How could God abandon all his children through the atrocities of this world? How do I explain his work to my congregation when I've lost my faith? I am worried because sooner or later they will notice this change in me; they are not stupid. I have become sullen and less approachable. I have less patience, and I fear I am failing my congregation and myself. I am not a perfect person and I am certainly a disappointment to God and my congregation. I live with this negativity everyday and have no one to talk to. Thankfully I am anonymous in this writing or my shame would envelop me...
> Pastor George

Pastor George is a painful example of a helper who has suffered an inner transformation of his own identity due to bearing witness to domestic violence, child abuse, death, rape, and other traumatizing events. He never realized that it is absolutely acceptable to have his own personal experience of feeling outraged, horrified, shocked, saddened, or vulnerable to attack. His shame over being human prevented him from seeking his own path of recovery, which would have helped him to remember that his normal human reactions need not sever him from his faith. Sadly, he left the church and suffered criticism from the congregation for abandoning them. On a more positive note, he sought counseling for his Vicarious Traumatization, reconnected with his spiritual self, and is considering returning to a new congregation.

Chapter Five: Countertransference and the Wounded Healer

When a professional is helping someone, there is a conscious and an unconscious part of the helping relationship. The conscious part of a helping relationship is the overt activity that goes on between the client and the helper. When someone comes for help, the helper simply gives that help in whatever way is appropriate for his or her designated profession (i.e., lawyer, doctor, therapist, etc.). An unconscious relationship dimension, called countertransference, affects every helping professional. Countertransference is the displacement of helper emotion onto the client or, as it is more generally identified, the helper's emotional involvement in the helping interaction (Earley, 2006).

This unconscious part can get away from us if left unaddressed and can cause a lot of pain for the client and the helper. At some level, every person we meet in our work reminds us of someone who impacted us at an earlier time in our own human development. Stored memories can become triggered and the feeling states connected to those memories can rise to the consciousness. Vicarious Trauma makes it exceedingly difficult to tune in to that second dimension of the helping relationship because Vicarious Trauma sufferers may be numbed, dissociated, distracted, or in denial of those unconscious parts of their own lives. While this countertransference phenomenon is considered a normal psychological process, it is important for helpers to have an awareness of it when it is happening so that they might help clients with integrity and accountability.

The other aspect of VT we need to address when discussing countertransference is the neurocircuitry behind it that stimulates hippocampal activity. Within the hippocampus is stored every memory in the life of an individual. If a helper is an adult survivor of childhood trauma, her or his own traumatic memories may be triggered, throwing the helper into an intense personal crisis (Wilson & Lindy, 1999). Helpers need to recognize their own internal reactivity and seek appropriate counsel and consultation to address this existential upset. Otherwise, it compromises their ability to address the issues of the client. Even worse, helpers are now at risk of acting-in or acting-out around their own painful historical triggers.

In cases where helpers are suffering from Vicarious Trauma, they may be unaware of their own countertransference issues because they are either consciously avoiding or unconsciously dissociating from the event. The danger this presents is that of helpers placing themselves in an incapable position; if they are unaware of their own personal reactions, helpers will be jaded in the responses they provide and their clients' best interests cannot be served (Wilson & Lindy, 2004).

As we stated previously, at least 53% of helping professionals report themselves to be trauma survivors; that percentage is most likely considerably shy of reality because many helpers are ashamed to embrace, much less report, their own trauma history. Unfortunately, this type of denial or repression leaves helpers at risk to experience a countertransference phenomenon.

One particular study surveyed over 500 clinicians and over 32% reported childhood sexual abuse histories (Pearlman & MacIan, 1995). Sexually abused therapists were more likely to report countertransference issues, especially boundary issues, than non-abused therapists. Successful boundary negotiation by a therapist involves efficient recognition of the emptiness and terror that a perceived threat to attachment can produce. The most common error in countertransference management with VT victims is a sudden and unexplained change in boundary rules. For example, consider the following case example submitted by Cherisse, a therapist who was an adult survivor of childhood abuse.

> This may sound like a small incident, but I found myself highly agitated when this situation would come up. I worked with a client named Louise who was an adult child of an alcoholic. She came to counseling to heal from being raised by a physically violent alcoholic mother. When Louise's mother would drink, she would become extremely violent and physically assault Louise. Her physical assaults usually included banging her head against the wall or upon a countertop. Louise's mother directed every aspect of her life. She never learned to function independently. She moved from life with an intrusive mother into a marriage with a tyrannical husband.
>
> Louise really had difficulty acknowledging her legitimate anger toward her mother and used pity as a substitute. Anger was a difficult emotion for Louise to negotiate and, at a young age, she got into passive aggressive expressions of her angry feelings. This was recreated in the therapeutic relationship by Louise running chronically late for our meetings. What I was unaware of

was that I was not protecting my own boundaries, something that has always been a challenge as a result of my own trauma history. Louise would be 15 minutes late for her appointment, the session would run 10 minutes over and I would feel angry that I was back-peddling for the rest of my day with my subsequent appointments.

One particular day, Louise showed up at 9:20 a.m. for her 9:00 a.m. appointment. Since her appointment should have been completed at 9:50 a.m. on this day I closed the session at exactly that time. Louise looked at her watch and challenged me that she did not have enough counseling time. I shared with her my interpretation of her chronic lateness and boundary issues exemplified by her misuse of time.

I realized through my anger at her that I was experiencing a countertransference phenomenon. I had allowed the client to intrude upon my boundaries of time management and this elicited an upset that had its roots in a much earlier time in my life. Luckily, I was conscious enough to notice the countertransference, identify it, and process it with the client as a catalyst for her own self-awareness and growth. The client initially appeared irritated at my boundary setting because it was a change from what she had grown accustomed to; however, after considering my explanation, she seemed calmer as she left the session. My client still runs at least 15 minutes late for her sessions, but now we end promptly at 10 minutes to the hour.
Cherisse, Licensed Professional Counselor

Fortunately, Cherisse was in touch with her own normal countertransference triggers, able to recognize her anger, process it internally, and label it as a boundary intrusion. She managed her own historical arousal of anger in a responsible and productive way through which the client gained some useful awareness for how she covertly expresses her own anger. Although, at the time of this writing, the client's behavior had not changed, she was able to understand, through the productive conversation shared with Cherisse, the impact that her behavior had on others and the importance of developing emotional maturity so that she might parent herself through effective time management.

Another example of countertransference is when a family lawyer is stressing to his female client the importance of achieving A's in her college courses because the client reminds him of his daughter who is living singly and trying to move forward in an independent lifestyle. His anxieties about his own daughter create a pathway to this countertransference with his client. The lawyer in this example is transferring his unconscious feelings to the client.

Countertransference is defined in opposition to transference, in which a client in a helping relationship begins to transfer feelings (whether positive or negative) to the professional. For example, a person in therapy may begin to look at the therapist as if the therapist were the patient's mother, transferring his or her feelings for the real mother to the therapist. While this is considered a positive sign in psychoanalytical therapy, showing that the patient is making progress, it also presents an emotional stressor for the therapist. Helpers who have not had counseling training may not recognize this transference and may act on it in a negative way. Developing insight and becoming educated about these transference/countertransference phenomena is essential if you are working in the helping professions.

Literature suggests that countertransference has the potential to be present in any helping relationship. The research states that it is often one of the biggest challenges for new helpers to overcome and, while there is no way to totally overcome the problem of countertransference (since as humans we all form opinions of others), learning to not let countertransference affect a helping relationship is key. Countertransference can also be seen as a useful phenomenon for helpers because it can allow them to gain insight into the kinds of emotions and reactions the client often tends to induce in others. In this way, countertransference is a welcomed phenomenon that can provide invaluable insight to the helping relationship (Kennedy, 1993).

According to Jay Earley (2006), the following are transference and countertransference patterns that any helper needs to be aware of. In order to reduce the potential for Vicarious Trauma, helpers need to be well informed and aware of their own countertransference issues and responses so that they can protect themselves from accumulating upsetting feeling states that begin to take their toll. Over time, the occupational hazards inherent in the helping professions will wreak havoc on helpers' health. It is happening every day, even though it is not visible or palpable. Awareness is your first line of defense.

NEEDY PATTERN

Transference:	Sees therapist as nurturing mother; dependent.
	Sees therapist as non-nurturing mother; hurt, angry.
Countertransference:	Overly involved in caring for client.
	Repulsed by client's needs.

NEED-DENYING PATTERN

Transference:	Denies need for nurturing or help from therapist.
Countertransference:	Happy that client doesn't need anything.

INSECURE PATTERN

Transference:	Afraid therapist is judgmental of her/him or doesn't like her/him.
Countertransference:	Overly involved in reassuring client.
	Repulsed by client's insecurities.

ISOLATED PATTERN

Transference:	Avoidance of personal/emotional relationship with therapist or denial of it.
Countertransference:	Treating relationship as if it were only instrumental.
	Moving too quickly to connect with the client.

COMPLIANT PATTERN

Transference:	Pretends that everything the therapist does works.
Countertransference:	Believes the client's compliance

DEFIANT PATTERN

Transference:	Refuses to cooperate with much of the therapy.
	Fights with therapist and criticizes therapist's approach.
Countertransference:	Feels ineffective and incompetent. Feels hurt by criticisms.
	Becomes frustrated with client; gets into arguments and power struggles with client.

PASSIVE-AGGRESSIVE PATTERN

Transference:	Experiences the therapist as pressuring her/him to perform.
	Consciously wants to please the therapist, but fails to do therapy correctly, or, if she/he does, fails to progress in life or denies progress. Unconsciously, this is an expression of anger at the therapist and an attempt to defeat the therapist, who she/he experiences as attempting to control and change her/him.
Countertransference:	Becomes frustrated with the client for failing. Feels ineffective and incompetent.

CONTROLLING PATTERN

Transference:	Refuses to allow therapist to do much; must be in control of the therapy.
Countertransference:	Gets into a power struggle with the client.

VICTIM PATTERN

Transference:	Complains to therapist about his/her misery in unconscious attempt to get therapist to fix his / her problems for him / her.
	Blames therapist for his/her problems for same unconscious reason.
Countertransference:	Fails to see victim stance and keeps trying to reassure and encourage client.
	Becomes angry and frustrated with client.

CODEPENDENT PATTERN

Transference:	Tries to take care of therapist. Picks up on clues of therapist's pain or life struggles and engages therapist in talking about them. Notices therapist's insecurities and assuages them.
Countertransference:	Allows client to take care of her/him.

SUSPICIOUS PATTERN

Transference: Suspects that the therapist harbors negative feelings toward him/her that are hidden or that the therapist will at some point turn on or abandon him/her. Doesn't trust positive things he/she sees.

Countertransference: Becomes annoyed at client for lack of trust and hides this from client, thereby making client's fears come true.
Pressures client to trust prematurely.

AGGRESSIVE PATTERN

Transference: Periodically becomes enraged at therapist over a certain behavior or situation that develops.
Criticizes the therapist's handling of the therapy.

Countertransference: Becomes frightened of client's anger and tries to avoid triggering it, leading to non-therapeutic behavior.
Becomes angry at client and shows it directly or covertly.
Feels hurt by criticism, leading to feelings of incompetence.
Argues with client about content of criticisms.

SELF-JUDGING PATTERN

Transference: Constantly blames herself/himself for poor performance in therapy and life. Often expects the therapist to feel the same way.

Countertransference: Tries to reassure client without directly working on the inner critic.
Becomes annoyed with client for constant self-judgment, thereby contributing to it.

CHARMING PATTERN

Transference: Entertains the therapist with fascinating stories; engages the therapist's sexual interest; charms the therapist.

Countertransference: Becomes more interested in the client's charm (in whichever form) than in engaging in therapy.

BRITTLE FORM OF DEFENSIVE PATTERN

Transference: Becomes deeply hurt by challenges from the therapist (or things perceived that way) and reacts with brittle defenses.

Countertransference: Tries to reassure the client without dealing with underlying issues.
Keeps going with the challenge.
Becomes frustrated that client can't deal with any challenges.

PRIDEFUL PATTERN

Transference: Expects therapist to appreciate or admire him / her.
Acts superior and demeaning toward therapist.

Countertransference: Therapist admires client or gives appreciation, thinking client needs support.
Therapist becomes angry at the client for grandiosity or condescension and challenges him/her in an unsupportive way.

ENTITLED PATTERN

Transference: Client expects special favors from therapist around money, time, and so on.
Client expects therapist to give him/her exactly what he/she wants.
In making these demands, the client completely disregards any needs or limits the therapist might have.

Countertransference: Therapist gives in to client's demands.
Therapist becomes angry at client's demands and at therapist's needs being ignored

Here is one testimonial and exceptional explanation from the viewpoint of a psychiatrist who did evaluations for the judicial system. Her story is posted on the Web under the name "Dr. Sanity" [drsanity.blogspot.com].

Some years ago I used to moonlight and perform psychiatric evaluations for the prosecutors and public defenders in the county where I lived. Personality disorders have always been an interest of mine, and you can find many examples in the jails and prisons.

One particular case stands out in my mind. I was asked by the public defender to evaluate a young man who was accused of murdering his girlfriend. The man was adamant that he was innocent and his lawyer wanted to believe him, but something didn't seem quite right to him, so he decided to ask me for my psychiatric opinion of his client and evaluate the possibility that there might be a psychiatric defense.

Steve was, to all intents and purposes, a model citizen in many ways. He held a responsible job, had no prior legal problems. He had been going with his girlfriend for about 3 months when her body was found in a wooded area, not too far from the apartment complex where he lived. Naturally, he was the prime suspect in her murder (she was strangled). There was also some physical evidence present that linked him to her death, but he insisted that she had left his apartment earlier that morning to go to work after spending the night with him and he had not seen her after that.

When I met with him, I experienced what we used to call in my medical school a "positive Gorney's sign," meaning that the hair on the back of my neck stood on end. It is a "gut feeling" that something very strange is going on, something that may not be readily obvious to a casual observer or on first inspection.

In my career, I have learned to respect such feelings. It almost always means that I need to look more closely at a patient and pay more attention to what they are saying or doing that might be stimulating my instinctive emotional response.

Occasionally, I find no corroborating evidence in their behavior for such feelings, and in those cases I simply file the emotional data away and make a conscious decision not to act on it for the time being. Sometimes I find negative evidence that contradicts my primal emotional response. Both situations are cues to me that I must try to figure out what it was that triggered my emotion, and the first step is to look within myself for an explanation. Does the patient remind me of someone I have ambivalent feelings about? Am I upset at something going on in my life? Am I having a bad day? Because it is important to realize that gut feelings can be communicating false data about others, but correct data about one's self.

A person's visceral response to another individual is usually based on mostly unconscious factors that are in play in the responder's life. To make an assessment of the gut feeling's appropriateness, the contents of the unconscious must be explored and brought to the conscious level and considered. Those unconscious internal conflicts can easily mask the inappropriate aspects of the feelings, making them worthless as a means of understanding the external world.

Taking this kind of action as a method of checking and understanding one's own feelings is a process called "insight" or "self-awareness." Some people do this quite naturally and honestly. Some learn in therapy or when they are in crisis. But if insight is absent, then one's feelings have the potential to do great harm, both to one's self and to others.

Some unconscious factors, or psychological defenses, that can make one's feelings untrustworthy are: 1) the person you are responding to has become symbolic of someone else in your life (displacement, fantasy, or perhaps distortion); 2) focusing on one particular aspect of a person, you ignore other, more objective data that are available to you about the person (denial); 3) you place your own unacceptable feelings onto the other person—e.g., I'm not an angry person, he's an angry person! (projection or full-blown paranoia).

The truth is that there are countless ways that unconscious processes within ourselves can distort our responses to others and to reality itself. Growing up and attaining maturity requires that we take a moment to consider such factors playing a role in our emotions before we act on those emotions. If we come to know ourselves and understand our own weaknesses, vulnerabilities, limitations, and secrets, then our emotional responses to people or to the world can be very valuable tools to help interpret the world. But they are only tools, and if not used wisely, they can do more harm than good. Feelings cannot be used in a court of law—for good reason. And they are not ultimate truth in the court of reality, either.

As I have gained experience in psychiatry, more often than not, when I trust such feelings and proceed to analyze what is bothering me about the situation, I discover a wealth of information that would have otherwise remained hidden. Sometimes that "wealth of information" is only about myself, but even in that case, I learn something new—frequently something insightful that I didn't want to know—about myself.

For example, I recently became aware that I was extremely annoyed and inappropriately angry at a 70-year-old woman who was not getting better in treatment because she refused to acknowledge that she had a severe drinking problem.

My anger at this sad, elderly lady was completely out of proportion to the situation—after all, I have numerous patients that do exactly the same thing, and their behavior does not typically bring out such intense feelings in me.

"Why doesn't she tell herself the truth?" I thought. Then I realized that this thought was what I used to verbalize with some anguish to my own mother—who died of her alcoholism at age 72, refusing all my entreaties to get help and treatment. My entire interaction with this elderly patient was all about my own unresolved anger and grief toward my mother's death and not about the patient at all. Once I appreciated that I had to deal with my issues separately and not force my patient into a role she hadn't asked for, I could respond to her for who she really was and maybe even help her. The reality was that she wasn't my mother, though my mind had made her so.

In psychiatry, we refer to feelings like those that I projected onto my patient as countertransference. We are generally aware that our own feelings are not always a reliable tool for interpreting reality. In fact, they may misdirect us or even completely interfere with our attempts to help another person.

What a person feels in a particular situation is also an incontrovertible fact, but it may or may not reveal any real information about the situation—and only reveal information about the person who is experiencing the feeling. To remember that this is the rule, rather than the exception about feelings, all we need do is to observe the chaotic lives of most of our patients, where thinking is almost always subsumed by emotion.

With all those caveats, it is still true that using one's own feelings as a clinical barometer can at times be very helpful. I am aware, for example, that I have a very reliable emotional reaction to those patients with borderline/narcissistic/antisocial personalities. To put it simply, I find myself feeling amused and entertained by patients with these personality traits.

This is in stark contrast to most of my colleagues, who generally come to feel extremely frustrated and angry at such patients. My emotional response is probably the reason why I don't get "burned out" professionally in dealing with these difficult patients, while many of my colleagues run like hell from them. So, when I am evaluating a person for the first time, and I find that I am responding in an amused fashion or if I have a feeling that I am being lied to or manipulated—or even if I sense that there is something I can't quite put my finger on—these emotional data points/reactions can add to the other evidence I collect in order to make specific diagnoses.

In contrast, when dealing with a depressed and passive patient, I frequently find myself responding to their plight with feelings of frustration and often experience a transient fantasy of wanting to shake the person and say, "This is your LIFE! Why are you wasting it?"

Clearly, I try to reign in this response since it is counterproductive and not particularly useful for my patient in their current state of emotional distress. But it can confirm the diagnosis of depression, if I had any doubt about it.

Now, back to Steve. My reaction to him was very revealing. Besides the sign I mentioned above, I found myself amused at his attempts to manipulate my response to him and began to suspect that there was a serious personality disorder behind the civilized facade that he presented. Although I felt he was trying a little too hard to convince me of his bona fides, I was impressed when he told me he had received a community award for rescuing a woman the year before.

He remained adamant about his innocence. I found that I didn't believe him, despite his obvious passionate protestations of innocence. I began to understand the unease that my attorney friend was having about the case, but after almost 2 hours of talking to Steve, I had no other data except for my gut feeling that he wasn't telling me the truth and my suspicion that I was dealing with someone with strong psychopathological personality traits at the least and a full-blown antisocial personality at the other extreme.

If my feelings had been the sole data point, I would have determinedly ignored them. To confirm my unease, I would have to search for some objective data to support my unease about Steve.

So I asked for the hundreds of pages of documents that are generated from a criminal investigation. These are the pages and pages of notes from the first policemen on the scene and the interviews of all the people connected with the case. Eventually I read the detective's notes from the first interview with Steve at the beginning of the case, before he became the prime suspect.

Interestingly, Steve apparently knew the detective who had interviewed him in this murder case, from a previous interaction with him almost a year ago. In our interview, I remembered that Steve had mentioned his positive feelings about the detective from their previous encounter and his optimism that evidence would be found exonerating him. Even more interestingly, this previous interaction with the detective was in connection to the event Steve briefly mentioned to me about earning a community award.

My gut feeling returned even stronger. THIS IS IMPORTANT! It was the message it transmitted to me. I immediately obtained records about the incident of one year ago, and here is the information as I pieced it together.

A year earlier, a woman jogger had been shot by a sniper. This crime had taken place fairly close to the apartment building that Steve had lived in at the time, near a park. Steve reportedly had also been jogging, heard the shot, and saw the woman fall. He immediately ran to her aid, calling 911 and then administering CPR and keeping the woman alive until help came. Sadly, the woman jogger later died of her wound in the hospital. But Steve was honored with a Good Samaritan award from the city. The police detective who interviewed him for that murder case was the same one that took his statement a year later in the murder of his girlfriend.

Do you begin to see where this gut feeling was taking me? This could most certainly be an amazing coincidence, but my gut feeling was telling me it wasn't a coincidence at all. On the contrary, my instinct—my feeling—told me this was no coincidence.

The police had not yet made the connection between the two cases (I have no doubt that they eventually would have, without my help). I called the detective and asked him if he remembered Steve. He did not. When I prompted him about the other case, there was a short silence, then a faint gasp.

That murder had never been solved. The detective assured me he would look into it, and sure enough, a few weeks later, he called me to report that they had found the sniper's gun for the previous crime in a locker at Steve's workplace. Steve's public defender had to fire me, since not only could I not help his current case, but I had implicated his client in another murder. If only Steve had not needed to tell me about his community award, a statement which didn't feel right in the context of our interview, then I probably would never have made the connection. But Steve provided the connection, and my emotional reaction to Steve motivated me to follow through and Steve's civilized cover was blown. He was eventually convicted of the woman jogger's murder as well as the strangulation of his girlfriend (which was motivated by her telling him she was pregnant). Police were actively looking into several other unsolved murders of young women in that area of the city to see if there could be any connection to Steve.

So, why am I telling this story? Because I believe that feelings are an extremely important resource all people have at their disposal for understanding the world around us. In some situations, the only thing we have to help us make decisions are our feelings. This is not the ideal, but sometimes it can suffice.

Humans are both feeling and thinking beings. If we ignore our feelings we have psychologically blinded ourselves to important information about the world, and if we ignore our mind and our reason, we have done the same thing. If we do not use both faculties together, we do not see the whole inner and outer world of reality.

The unquestioning reliance on one's feelings as the be-all and end-all of perceiving reality has some MAJOR, MAJOR snags associated with it. It leads to chaotic, dysfunctional relationships, instability, histrionic and impulsive behavior, and a lack of concern for the needs and feelings of other people.

It has been my experience that many people have a sort of primitive, child-like reverence for whatever they feel. That's all they know and all they need to know, seemingly. They never bother to try to understand why they feel the way they do, or even to objectively understand the source feelings. Indeed, it isn't always necessary to do so, but for many, living has become a matter of 'I feel, therefore I am.'

Well, I am here to tell you that this is the motto of the Steves of the world—who function exclusively on the basis of their feelings—and who have no room or inclination to bother with anybody else's feelings or needs. Why the Steves of the world are all wrapped up in themselves and their feelings, and why, despite their verbalizations to the contrary, they are truly incapable of the empathy with other people.

Empathy, or the ability to feel what others are feeling, is actually a healthy form of psychological projection, but (and this is a very important "but") it is projection with high degree of personal insight and sensitivity to one's self as well as to others." (Dr. Pat Santy, 2006)

Dr. Santy's narrative is an intensive explanation of the delicate balance between the thinking and feeling aspects of working with a client. Professionals must have the insight for self-examination when they find themselves experiencing personal feeling states about the client's story or behavior. Countertransference can take a very destructive turn in the helping relationship if the helper is struggling with VT. Here is a submission from a lawyer who has worked in the field of family law for over 30 years.

I have been a family law attorney for over 30 years. I represent only women in divorce cases and encounter many who have little, if any experience in managing their own financial affairs. When I first started in this field, it was hard for me not to be judgmental of these women. Maybe that's because my own wife is a very capable and highly successful businessperson. She is strong, decisive, and fiercely independent. It's funny that I ended up building a practice that focused on representing exactly the opposite kind of gal.

The case that stuck with me over many years is the one that involved a lady named Belle. Belle was married for 38 years and had four children. She was a society lady of sorts, with a butler, two housekeepers, and a groundskeeper. She even had a chauffeur and a chef. She wanted for nothing. Her husband had an affair with a younger woman and filed suit for a divorce. Belle completely fell apart. She appeared in my office with barely the ability to speak; she was shaking with anxiety and couldn't figure out how she would survive without Harvey. She lamented that Harvey took care of everything: the bills, the house, the vacation planning, even picked out her wardrobe and had it sent directly to the home. He planned all the social events and made her life seem like it came out of a fairy tale. She could not understand what she did wrong.

Over the course of time I worked with her, it appeared I was her surrogate husband. She called for every decision, including what to wear for the first court appearance. She came to the office with several "appropriate" selections for my perusal.

I found myself growing more and more irritated with what I perceived to be her meaningless phone calls and idiotic questions. One particular afternoon, I finally took her call after refusing to respond to the first 10. She wanted to know what time she should have her chauffer pick her up from our first settlement conference scheduled for the next morning. I felt a strong visceral reaction. My heart was pumping and my breathing was heavy. I was literally seeing stars. I told her I would have to call her back about the time, just so that I could take a moment and compose myself. I almost slammed the phone down at the end of that call. I frightened myself with my reaction. I had to take some time and get introspective.

What the hell was going on?! Why was this call different from all the others? I decided to call this psychologist who I regularly use as a professional witness in divorce cases and shared with him the exaggerated reaction I was having with this client. We went to college together, so he knows me pretty well. He started to laugh. I told him that I didn't think it was funny.

After he apologized, he reminded me of when, back in college, my parents were divorcing and how my mother tormented me daily with phone calls and streams of questions about the minutia of her life. But what he remembered most was my impatience and disappointment in her lack of ability to pull

herself up and take charge of her life. He explained transference and countertransference to me and he told me it was normal. He also reminded me to deal with my own "historical irritation" and leave it out of the client-attorney relationship. I realized then, if I needed to set a boundary with Belle, I should take a half hour with her and nicely do just that."
Stanley, Family Law Attorney

Stanley was fortunate to have so readily at hand a mental health professional he was comfortable consulting and who could reframe his agitation into something meaningful and productive. Many helping professionals either do not have that luxury or are fearful and resistant to ask for help. Instead, they have a countertransference reaction and have to repress it, experience the brain strain, and endure how that strain affects their physiology and their psyche.

Remember that countertransference is considered normal in that any helping relationship can take on the unconscious undertone of a surrogate family system. For example, if you are helping someone whose personality reminds you of a critical parent, your brain activity will include stimulation of the hippocampus (memory center) and those historical neurons will travel your brain just as if you were a child again, standing before that parent and having all the uncomfortable feeling states you had with that parent long ago. The necessity around this phenomenon is to face and turn into, as opposed to avoid, these normal reactions and body memories so that they may be acknowledged and respected for what they truly are and to utilize them to be of help rather than hindrance to the client.

Chapter Six: The Miracle Worker Reverie

T he Miracle Worker Reverie is an altered state of consciousness helpers unwittingly enter into in order to counteract their unconscious experience of the most foundational symptoms of Vicarious Trauma: compromised safety and self-esteem needs. After years of witnessing secondary trauma with controlled empathy, helpers frequently find themselves compromised physically, emotionally, and spiritually without recognizing that they are suffering from Vicarious Trauma. The affliction of untreated VT plummets professional helpers into a bitter transition in their world-view. As a result, helping professionals are at great risk for only feeling good when they perceive themselves as miracle workers, effecting amazing solutions and making huge dramatic life changes for the client.

Helpers, in their own mind and the mind of the client, become god-like and omnipotent. This thinking is in direct opposition to a healthy world-view or spiritual outlook. Taking on this type of miracle worker persona is an unhealthy defense that helpers believe counterbalances their deteriorative view of the world. Vicarious Trauma deforms helpers' view of the world into a dark, unsafe, nasty place; an angry, threatening place; a place where life as they know it can be taken away with a board complaint or a lawsuit from an unhappy client. There is no trust, there is no hope, and there is no faith.

As an alternate way of dealing with their compromised esteem needs, helpers go into the Miracle Worker Reverie, which becomes the inverse mind state that counteracts feeling like a powerless, flawed human being. Unfortunately, helpers are addressing the problem by creating another problem.

The treatment of VT demands that we examine our motivation for engaging in this type of work. We need to understand that we tend to cope by turning off our own negative feeling states. One convoluted way to contain these negative feelings and perceptions is to compensate by becoming Miracle Workers. This is a method of distraction from VT; helpers feel exalted and put on a pedestal by the client, or helpers feel exalted and put themselves on a pedestal in their own minds. At this point, one of the compelling reasons to remain in our role as a professional helper is for the "payback" of feeling euphoric, profound ecstasy by believing we perform acts of supernatural quality for another person. Unfortunately, there is nothing spiritual about it; it is actually ego-driven. This is a posturing of superiority that covers a damaged and extremely vulnerable concept of self.

The problem here is that the true nature of the therapeutic alliance that is built upon rapport, trust, and positive regard is superseded by the helper's need for power, control, and superiority in order to maintain the reverie. This robs clients of their therapeutic right to have their healing put in their own hands. Helpers often keep their clients in therapy or in protracted litigation, not for the client's benefit, but for the benefit, either emotional or financial, of helpers themselves. The belief is that if helpers discharge clients, they may not be able to make it on their own; they may need helpers to survive and make good decisions. In other words, helpers will save them because they cannot save themselves. It is important for helpers to view the client from a strength perspective so as not to give the perception that the client is incapable of handling the material of the helping interaction on their own.

One of the most significant dangers in what we are referring to is that, as this compulsive behavior pattern continues, helpers are unaware of their limitations in serving clients. When helpers are lost in the Miracle Worker Reverie, they do not see the benefit of referring clients out to more competent helpers or terminating with clients because treatment is complete. Clients then begin to serve the ego needs of helpers and the clients' treatment is severely compromised. The Miracle Worker Reverie can seduce a helper into losing professional perspective, forgetting spiritual point of view, and increasing the risk for bad practice or practice outside the helper's level of expertise.

Here is a sobering account of one psychiatrist's experience with this phenomenon:

> I no longer practice medicine, and I've learned it was all of my own doing. I've come to understand where I went wrong and how I could have had the life I dreamed of and actually lived for a short time, until I lost perspective and forfeited a fantastic opportunity.

I was one of two child and adolescent psychiatrists in my area—well-trained, well-respected, and launching a new private practice. I took a huge risk to buy a building and launch a psychiatric practice based on the hope that things would work out in a positive manner. I hired exceptional administrative and professional staff to work with me so that the client experience from beginning to end was stellar. Soon I developed an intricate professional network—I built an excellent professional reputation and gathered many referrals from numerous resources throughout my community.

I was working very hard and seeing triple what was considered to be a normal caseload. I quickly was seen as the doctor for hopeless cases—and many resistant and difficult-to-treat cases were sent in my direction. I welcomed them all. I was working 100-hour weeks, but at the time, perceived it to be extraordinary because I could buy vacation homes, fancy cars, artwork, boats, even a private jet for my family's personal use. My wife and children spent summers at the beach and I worked day and night to pay for their comfort.

Now, in retrospect, I cannot believe the burden of caseloads I was shouldering and the internalization of horrific patient narratives I was suffering from. I was playing God and, from this position of power, I was building my kingdom. I'm not exactly sure when my relationships broke down, or when my grandiosity took over, but I found myself alone, isolated, and binging on seeing more and more patients to make myself feel powerful and revered. I noticed my staff beginning to complain about their workloads, which I either ignored or minimized. I fired those who could not keep up with my expectations. I became so over-focused on building a huge practice that I became much less attentive to important ethical aspects of maintaining such a practice.

A primary example of this was my attitude toward insurance claims and the filing thereof. I complained bitterly that my staff weren't getting their patients in often enough for therapy and that the billings were down. Eventually fraudulent insurance claims were filed. I created my own prison in that with all my power came a pervasive isolation. I was a prisoner of my own success. I felt I couldn't ask others for support, supervision, or input on a case. I was the great and brilliant psychiatrist. How could I ask for help?

I am not proud of what happened to me. I lost my practice, my family, my reputation, and my medical license. I spent years in treatment with a psychiatrist who understood the concept of VT. It is no excuse, but had I understood the damaging impact of working too hard and internalizing years worth of traumatic stories, I might have stayed more conscious of my own limitations. At the time, I distracted myself from this realization by seeing myself as omnipotent and building myself an empire. I believed I could save all those patients—I was the only one who could do it and I let them all down—but worse, I let myself and my family down. It's been a long road back.

Thomas, Psychiatrist

The ego-driven compulsion behind the helping professions needs to be understood and addressed. Thomas was driven by the power of the financial, emotional, professional, and egotistical rewards of his successes in being seen as a miracle worker. His loss of perspective was his downfall. The inability to debrief his traumas led him to distract himself and become overzealous in his quest for greatness. His ability to prioritize became negatively affected and his professional judgment suffered. He lost sight of his original motivation, which was to become a psychiatrist to serve people suffering with emotional disorders. As a result, he lost everything, including his giving human spirit. His addiction to helping, which was about him, prevented him from being a true agent of growth and change for his patients. His compulsion for helping was ultimately not for the benefit of the clients; it became his own personal addiction, with the payback never being quite enough, much like a drug. Drugs wear off after awhile and the user needs more (recognition), and more (money), and more (power). Worse, the tolerance for the pain from the stories we hear becomes higher and higher and the Vicarious Trauma intensifies unknowingly until it has destroyed its victim.

Chapter Seven: Rapid Advance Process for Vicarious Trauma Relief

Now that we have become aware of the many factors that set the stage for helping professionals to fall prey to the misery of Vicarious Trauma, it is time to discuss an effective brief approach to its treatment. We have talked about how neuroscience demonstrates that chronic stress injures and changes the structure of the brain. The strain of Vicarious Trauma also inhibits neurogenesis, or the birth of new neurons. VT victims in recovery need to recognize that new brain cells can come into a complicated, ingrained, and negative brain circuitry and become part of the circuitry in a restorative way (Begley, 2007).

Since we have come to understand that the brain damage of VT is experienced as a painful inner transformation in the individual's identity, perhaps the greatest negative impact can be described as a break to the essence or the spirit of the individual. After internalizing trauma content stories over time through the strain of controlled empathy, it should not be surprising that helping professionals finds themselves poor or broken in spirit. The core spiritual identity, the basic essence, becomes inaccessible.

The spirit of a helping individual can be identified as the level of consciousness that rises above upset and stress and responds to negative situations with dynamics such as courage, faith, hope, trust, and forgiveness. The neurocircuitry of trauma makes accessing the higher brain without a conscious and concerted effort very challenging. When people are in disconnect from this powerful higher perspective, they are left with primitive brain reactions such as fear and anxiety as their primary context for perceiving the world. They become stuck in self-definition that is negative and judgmental.

Vicarious Trauma leaves the individual at great risk to be in separation from the spiritual perspective or the higher brain. An individual's sense of spiritual identity is sacred unto itself and is free from self-judgment. Vicarious Trauma puts the helper in the position of self-regard that attacks the fundamental nature of helpers and states: "I am powerless; I am depressed; I am all powerful; I am a god." Treatment must include a viable method for bridging to the higher mind so helpers can remain healthy, centered, open, neutral, and positive in their work. Vicarious Trauma precipitates an Impasse in a helper's Spiritual Bridge or neural pathway to that higher level of consciousness. Recovery from VT must include some way to mend that Impasse and restore the neural pathway to the higher left-brain or the spiritual perspective.

The Rapid Advance model consists of five steps for VT recovery:

1. Reveal the History.
2. Recognize the Impasse.
3. Release the Past.
4. Respond to Fear.
5. Reconnect with the Spirit.

Reveal the History
It Was

It has been established that over 53% of helping professionals have reported themselves as trauma survivors. We can estimate that the actual number is higher than that since many helpers do not disclose their own trauma histories. Most helping professionals are highly skilled at controlled empathy because they have survived their own trauma histories and have become proficient at exercising emotional control. They have also developed a high tolerance for trauma content. Nonetheless, consciousness of what is going on for them unconsciously is critical in warding off the insidiousness of VT. The countertransference phenomenon can only be brought to consciousness by revealing the helper's own history, which is being stimulated in the hippocampus and amygdale of the helper's brain as the story of the client is unfolding.

The helping professional, like everyone else, has a very important and revealing personal history called childhood. Time must be taken to seriously consider and to study it. Many helpers have forgotten much of their own past or have developed selective recall about it. Now, we're not suggesting that a professional become bogged down in the past; far from it. Instead, we are suggesting that they review the past and use it as a catalyst to counteract the effects of countertransference, which leads to Vicarious Trauma. We are not suggesting that the past was all bad. The good stuff simply is not our concern right now. What we are interested in is how your memory of some upsetting events may be at risk of being triggered through your work, thereby incurring some breaks or

Impasses in your own **Spiritual Bridge,** or neural pathways to the higher mind. This Impasse negatively affects your belief system, core identity, and inner sense of well-being. It interferes with your ability to function at optimum level in your profession.

As helping professionals we know that children are considered "impressionable" because, when they first enter the world, they are almost entirely spiritual self and very much centered in the present. Babies have virtually no sense of the intellectual, physical, or emotional selves. As infants begin to move through the oversized, scary world, the other three soon begin to develop. This, for the most part, is as it is supposed to be, except when the higher brain or the spiritual self, which only knows acceptance, innocence, goodness, and love, is sacrificed to the development of the physical, emotional, and intellectual selves. The development of the physical, intellectual and emotional selves at the sacrifice of the spiritual self is also called the ego. When children develop an ego, they are converting to a fear-based way of thinking that is virtually opposed to the powerful spiritual component. This unconscious process happens to all of us. That's just the way it is. As we develop into adulthood the brain submerges painful memories deep within the hippocampus and we become like an onion with layers of defense over these disturbing memories.

Some people appear to be more separated from their spiritual selves than others. The depth of the Impasse or break in the **Spiritual Bridge** depends on the intensity of the historical fear to which the child was initially subjected. What you will come to understand is that no matter how wide the gap, reconnecting is equally easy for everyone. You simply need to acknowledge that the break did, in fact, occur, it recurs through your work, and then make the personal commitment to reconnect.

Unfortunately, too many of us remain unaware of unconscious reactions to clients' trauma content. That's why you are reading this book; to become consciously aware of what is unconsciously going on so that you may have a form of personal and professional empowerment. When helpers are in a place where an historical fear is unconsciously triggered, it can be torturous. The inclination of helpers is not unlike the predicament of Superman. Superman was a miracle worker; all powerful, as long as he was out of the range of Kryptonite. If Kryptonite was close by, he could still function as long as it was enclosed in lead. Our personal historical fears are our emotional Kryptonite. Our denial, in whatever form it takes, is the lead box. We operate powerfully as helpers until some traumatic client story we absorb flips the lid open on the lead box. Then watch out! We are at risk of feeling threatened and personally paralyzed and powerless.

Now, some of you may be saying, "This is hopeless. How could I ever overcome the constant risk of being traumatized through going to work?" Don't worry; that feeling of hopelessness is a great indicator of your own separation from your higher brain. Remember that hope is a higher mind, spiritually based behavior. It is easy to get back to hopefulness.

The intensity of the negative historical experience triggered is actually irrelevant. An historical experience is a memory and nothing more. It lurks around in the recesses of our minds. It simply does not exist in the present. The particular meaning of any memory is the meaning we choose to ascribe to it. We can change the meaning at any time. You'll have to decide when you are ready to change the meaning of a memory. But first you'll have to acknowledge it.

Reframing a painful past experience in terms of a spiritual break motivates us to change its impact. Once you can accept that the force of VT precipitates a separation from the higher mind, reconnecting is similarly restorative for everyone. Operating from the spiritual perspective of self-acceptance, rather than the ego-based perspective of fear, restores us as helpers to our original transparent identity and places a painful event, be it the client's or our own, in the position of nothing more than a statement of what was.

Your personal history is important to keep in mind as you work because it is where you began to make judgments about yourself and your place in the world as you moved through those early experiences. It was the decision-making place for what became the objects of your faith: for what you believe and for what you have unconsciously set up and lived out through the course of your life. Conscious or not, your childhood experiences are triggered through the course of your work. Your childlike reactions to trauma content are also triggered. This creates a brain strain on the primitive and mid portions of the brain, where raw feelings emerge. If you are working a lot, you probably have a neural pattern that prohibits you from accessing your higher mind, as a way of providing some healing, comforting thoughts, and emotions.

Recognizing the Impasse
It Is

History repeats itself. We can remember many times when we, as children, swore to ourselves that we would never say to our children some of the inane things our mothers and fathers said to us. We humble ourselves before you now as we confess to the number of times we have nearly had to gag ourselves in order not to say to our kids *exactly* what our mothers and fathers said to us! Similarly, those who have unresolved fear about the past are doomed to repeat it. We repeat it in our primary relationships, in our parenting, in the workplace, and in our friendships. The tendency to do this is unconscious, yet seductive and addictive; we will actually attract personality types into our experiences that are easy targets for the projection of our childhood fears.

So let's take a trip down memory lane and look closely at where you have been. You've been in your Mother's womb, in her arms, and in the arms of others. You were really small when the rest of the world seemed really big, and your little eyes perceived many things as larger than life itself. You have probably forgotten about all that over the years. To quickly remember, simply take a second, put the book down, squat close to the floor, and look all around you. Quite a different perspective, wouldn't you say? Have you ever visited a kindergarten or first grade classroom? The chairs and desks are so tiny, so close to the floor. The drinking fountain lies low as well. You perceived early that certain things, certain people, certain places were scary and you didn't like that feeling of fear, so you buried it. A child automatically does this as a survival mechanism. After all, how can a defenseless child survive in a scary world? He can't.

So, in order to keep away from the feeling of fear, you began to develop certain *acting-in* or *acting-out* behaviors as a way to distract yourself from unpleasant feelings. You might have sucked your thumb, had nightmares, or wet the bed. Perhaps you had temper tantrums, were painfully shy, or were aggressive with other children. Maybe you did poorly in school or not as well as you might have. Maybe you got sick a lot. Conceivably, you were too competitive or not competitive enough. These behaviors served as distractions from the unpleasant feeling of fear.

Take a minute to recall some of your childhood traits and behaviors. They were the seedlings of traits and behaviors you possess today. Some of them are great. Some are huge obstacles in the way of you remembering who you really are. An understanding of how they evolved empowers you to decide, in the present, which were useful and which were not.

The self-protective distractions of our childhood "mature" as we develop. A thumb sucker may develop into an alcohol/drug abuser. A painfully shy child may develop into a depressed adult. A wounded child might develop into a savior. Although these are a little more sophisticated, they are distractions all the same, and we re-create the past with the help of our distractions. Once our history has been revealed, we are able to get conscious about or recognize how we repeatedly find ourselves at the Impasse in adulthood and more so through our work.

Fear-based relationships can be further explored by looking at Dr. Eric Berne's (1964) Drama Triangle. The Drama Triangle is drawn from Berne's concept of Transactional Analysis. Visualize, if you will, a triangle with three different roles at each point. One role is the victim position, the next is the rescuer position, and the third is the perpetrator position. When we are stuck in a fear-based perspective, we are at risk of moving around this dysfunctional system with our clients, continually interchanging the roles.

DRAMA TRIANGLE

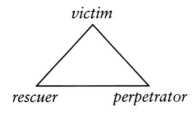

A medical doctor, James came to see us because he said he was having marital problems. There were problems all along in the 4 years he was with Krista, but things had really escalated when she got the phone bill and found out that he had made a series of calls to a 1-800 phone porn service. Krista shoved the bill at James and told him to get some help or she was filing for divorce.

James wasn't very enthused about working with us at first because he was very ashamed of his "presenting problem." He also saw himself as a "Miracle Worker" who ran a huge clinic for the poor. He was above needing help and, furthermore, he felt like he was being bullied by his wife into seeking treatment.

We pointed out to him that he was a very bright man and he certainly knew that he would be caught when the phone bill arrived. We interpreted the acting-out behavior not so much as a sexual addiction, but as a clear cry for some help. James listened to hundreds of traumatic stories at work and never considered the possibility of Vicarious Trauma. James felt relieved when it was put that way and he began to talk.

James overworked at the clinic and saw many people who were chronically ill because of traumatic circumstances: no homes, no money, hard drugs, rape, and assault. One patient, in particular, preyed on his mind constantly. She would come to the clinic no less than four times a week with many maladies that were the result of very poor living conditions and very poor nutrition. James would spend a great deal of time being a compassionate ear for this woman. She had given birth to a son seven years ago as a result of being raped by someone she knew in her tenement. She didn't care for this child due to the circumstances of his creation. The habit she formed to avoid taking care of him was by being chronically ill herself and incapacitated in her role as mother.

James was a quiet, gentle kind of guy who tended to keep to himself. Of course, the more he kept to himself, the more the story of the chronically ill lady rolled around in his mind. He became shut down in his marriage. The more shut down he became, the more his wife came after him, complaining that she did not receive enough love, affection, or intimacy.

James shared with us that he would really dissociate when Krista got sick. If she had a cold or the flu, rather than be helpful, he would be indifferent. This really sent his wife into orbit. Rather than helping his poor wife out, James felt put upon by Krista to take responsibility for her health. He resented her being ill. He distracted himself by becoming depressed. Finally, he chose a more covert way to express his anger to his wife. His attempt to get her attention worked. James was putting his marriage and his career at risk with his porn phone calls. He was a victim of Vicarious Trauma and he didn't even know it.

Revealing the history really helped us to get a handle on the situation. James was the last-born, only male in a family of three children. His mother was an "invalid" who was chronically sick—in bed most of the time and very powerful in her supine position. To this day, no one is certain about exactly what is wrong with her. James' father dedicated his entire life to nursing the woman, and her poor health set the tone for how the family system would evolve. The children were expected to keep quiet and take care of themselves lest his Mother have a setback. His Father had no needs in the marriage because it would be absurd to expect anything from a partner who was unable to function. James recalled feeling cheated and ignored as a child. He had no relationship with his mother and was more of a parent to his father in being cooperative with his Father's need to play nurse. This was the memory embedded in James's hippocampus.

James recognized the Impasse to his higher brain that got triggered by his relationship with the chronically ill woman at the clinic. Choosing to become a doctor seems logical after we reveal his own history. He also recognized how the drama triangle had unconsciously been created in his life. Working at the clinic made him vulnerable to VT.

His acting-in distraction of depression and his acting-out distraction of phone sex helped keep James dissociated from some very painful historical feelings that were being triggered by his work. He postponed having this upset for many years. Not surprisingly, James did not give much consideration to his spiritual identity and he reported doing nothing in the way of nurturing his Spiritual Self. That didn't surprise us. You can't nurture something to which you are not connected. Maternal abandonment, no matter what form it takes, is a severe break to the *Spiritual Bridge* or the neural pathway to the higher brain. James went from an innocent sense of identity to "I am abandoned and I am unworthy." James could not trust women; he had no faith in healthy love; he did not have the courage to state his position and ask to have his needs met; and last, but not least, he was prohibiting himself from accessing forgiveness because he had not yet acknowledged his anger, sadness, and shame. James looked calm and happy, but behind the gentle exterior was a very angry and sad man.

Once we recognize the Impasse triggered by Vicarious Trauma, we also notice that we basically move around in a constant state of separation anxiety. Traditionally, separation anxiety is a term that refers to the upset a child feels when he/she must detach from a parent. We believe that all anxiety is actually separation anxiety, since we define separation anxiety as the chronic underlying distress we feel as a result of being separated from the most loving and nurturing *spiritual* part of ourselves. This sensitivity is as unpleasant in adulthood as it is in childhood and we stick to certain distractions as a way to avoid feeling it. Separation anxiety would keep us trapped inside the Drama Triangle, a fear-based system. Recognizing and meeting this anxiety enables us to get out of the triangle entirely.

Those of us attached to the past are bound to unconsciously re-create it. We've been doing it for so long; we don't even notice it anymore. It also carries an addictive quality. The familiarity of being stuck there has a perverse sense of comfort simply because we are so connected to the associated unpleasant feeling states. Recognizing when we are replaying an updated version of an historical scene and experiencing rather than avoiding the separation anxiety that gets triggered in the replay are some very important skills in mending the *Spiritual Bridge*. *Recognizing the Impasse* is the wake-up call to do something different. Experiencing our separation anxiety motivates us to consciously work on reconnecting to the higher brain. When we reconnect to the Spiritual Self, we realize that we are never abandoned and therefore never alone. Resolving feelings of isolation is a powerful counterpoint to the symptoms of Vicarious Trauma.

Releasing the Past
I Can

Our unconscious attachment to some aspect of a painful past prohibits our bridging to the Spiritual Self. This self is an inner consciousness that stays peacefully centered in the here and now. Having to this point determined an Impasse and decided to no longer retreat from it, we can begin to mend the break in our *Spiritual Bridge*. This is experienced as a challenge because we are in the midst of Vicarious Trauma and separation anxiety at the time we call upon ourselves to begin the repair. Traditional psychology would coin this "free-floating anxiety." It is free-floating in that, as we let go of our denial and defensiveness, we fear drifting off into oblivion due to disconnection. We can now take a leap of faith in that, in letting go, we give ourselves back to our higher mind and protect ourselves from the danger of VT.

When we release the past, we release ourselves to exchange our purpose. As we give fear over to a higher form of thinking, we receive spiritually based dynamics in ourselves. When we exchange our purpose, we change our mind from separation through fear to connection through hope and peacefulness. We transform the objects of our faith by no longer inspiring the painful past through the trauma stories of others. Unpleasant feeling states are no longer the foundation of our beliefs. Instead, the higher mind, the *Spiritual Self*, is where we extend ourselves to keep vigil. We begin to form more healing neural pathways and can negotiate trauma material more resourcefully.

What exactly is the past? Webster's dictionary gives: "the time before or time gone by." What does that mean? The past is a span of time. Is it tangible? We don't think so. Our memories of times gone by are all that really exist and they exist only in our minds. Memories are not really the past per se; they are only perceptions of it. It is important to realize that what we remember has far less impact than how we remember it. The historical action is over. It is only our judgment of it that actually remains. In a family, a parent's memory may be very different from a child's. For example, a mother might perceive the family as having been wonderful, with her role as parent as having been very positive and helpful. A child of that mother may perceive the opposite. The child may have perceived it as unsafe, with that same mother as a scary woman! Who was right and who was wrong? Neither, yet both. In many situations, a child's release from historical pain is found in the understanding that *his or her* memory of Mom's behavior was his or hers own alone. Adult children can exchange their purpose from fear to *forgiveness* and in so doing relinquish the self-judgment that, in light of a painful memory, they were unworthy of receiving love.

The point is that a perception of the past exists in your mind and that is all there is left of it. The events themselves are much less meaningful than how you absorbed the events as they occurred. How you took them in, experienced them, processed them, and judged yourself in their context is what makes up your perception of them. You can change your perception any time you choose to relinquish judgment. When you reframe your perception of the past, you transform your neural circuitry around the memory, thereby releasing it.

Now, we realize that there are many people at the Impasse and who use their perceptions of the past as the objects of their faith; we can hear the balking: "Right, Vicki and Ellie. My father called me a whore and a slut; I have a faulty perception of that verbal abuse!" Yes, your father *did* verbally abuse you and it appears he's still doing it, only now he has your permission to do so. You see, the verbal attack no longer exists. Only your perception of it remains. It is important to grasp that the attack itself never had any meaning. The way you felt at the time it happened imparts the only meaning the attack has. How did you feel when you were being attacked? Scared, sad, angry, and shameful are words that probably describe your feelings. What have you done about those feelings? Distracted yourself through some acting-in or acting-out behavior that includes healing the pain of others.

Furthermore, you are at risk of taking that painful perception of the past and projecting it onto people and circumstances today in a counterproductive fashion. This can happen to you within the helping relationship through the phenomenon of countertransference. Those negative historical feelings are still there and, because you don't attend to them, you are stuck with a perception of the past that undoubtedly gets played out again and again in the here and now. So your father still verbally abuses you; only now he has your permission to do so. Such complicity is not the healthy, healing way to deal with a painful history.

Forgiveness, which is the relinquishment of historical judgment followed by a thought of peace, is the binding material of the *Spiritual Bridge*. It is the stuff that keeps the bridge intact as a span to the higher brain or Spiritual Self. Without forgiveness, there will always be an Impasse in the Bridge, making it impossible to connect to our greatest internal resource in the struggle against Vicarious Trauma. *Releasing the Past* requires the first step of forgiveness. *Responding to Fear* requires the second.

Forgiveness includes the correction of one's perception through the relinquishment of judgment. The events of our past and the past of our clients are not the obstacle in letting go; rather, it is our repeated decision to cast judgment on ourselves and the people connected to the events that detain us in it, sometimes for a lifetime. The choice to judge someone as good or bad, right or wrong, starts with judging ourselves.

Kayleigh, a social worker, came to our center because she was having difficulty shaking off a deep depression she reported having since she heard the devastating client story about the serious illness of the client's first child. The client noticed this child was not thriving shortly after he was born. A heart defect went undetected at birth. The client was on social services because of poverty and was really struggling to get some medical care for her baby. By the time she got in to see Kayleigh, the baby was seriously ill. Kayleigh was highly anxious as she battled the red bureaucratic tape of the government. Kayleigh noticed her depression deepening every time she met with this client.

We were able to quickly identify the countertransference. Kayleigh herself had a son named Todd. Todd, at the tender age of 17, died from heart failure while attending school. He originally had two holes in his heart at birth. He was operated on at 2 years old to repair the holes and when the doctors started his heart back up, it would not beat on its own. They implanted a pacemaker that seemed to do the trick. Todd lived a "normal" life till he keeled over in class.

Kayleigh shared in her third session that she was the firstborn to a very shaming, controlling mother. When Kayleigh entered adolescence, her mother began to attack her regarding her behavior with boys. Rather than sit and have an informative talk about the birds and the bees, she threatened Kayleigh about promiscuity and suggested to her daughter that she was provocative and "loose" with pubescent young men. Kayleigh finally embodied her Mother's theme by becoming pregnant at 16 years old. The young man involved with the pregnancy brought Kayleigh a "morning after pill" when she told him the news. He advised her that when she took the pill, she would begin to bleed and she would lose the pregnancy. Kayleigh was so terrified to be pregnant and judged as shameful she swallowed the pill. Nothing happened. Kayleigh met someone on the beach a few weeks later. He married her and claimed the pregnancy as a result of their marriage. Todd was born with a major birth defect. Kayleigh blamed herself and when Todd died from a broken heart, she began distracting herself from this devastation by helping others.

The first session we met with Kayleigh, she made a comment about the unattractive placement of the furniture. Shortly thereafter, she remarked angrily that Ellie was looking out the window. The second session, she began to preempt feedback by saying things like, "Now don't go saying any of that stupid

'You are a good person and you're OK' psycho-garbage to me!" Vicki took in a relaxing breath as I looked at her and responded, "Kayleigh, I wasn't going to say anything of the sort. I am having a reaction and I need to take a risk with you. My perception of some of your behaviors in building a relationship with us is that you are trying to connect to us in shame. Some judgmental remarks have tipped us off to this style. If you are being judgmental with us, then we imagine that you must be very judgmental with yourself. Perhaps this is a style you re-create from mother's role modeling." Kayleigh settled into her chair. "Yes," she said, "I am just like her and I hate myself for it." She had a confused expression on her face as we remarked, "So, are you now judging yourself for being judgmental?" She laughed for the first time since we had met and its tone was melodious. "I sure am, aren't I?"

Then we all laughed together, as some healing was taking place. When we are fearful and separated, we tend to beat on ourselves unmercifully. We need to remember that our purpose here on earth is certainly not to abuse ourselves.

When we are in a state of fear and shame we cannot access the neutrality of spiritual thinking. When we are connected to the higher mind, we realize that we should not judge the client's behaviors or our own and that we cannot do so. In giving up judgment, we merely give up what we never had a right to in the first place. Furthermore, when we operate from the higher mind, we can observe things from a higher consciousness that knows no separation. Through spiritual exercise, neural activity intensifies in the prefrontal cortex and we can utilize these restored pathways to find the intrinsic meaning behind our own suffering and the suffering of others. This healing replaces the ineffective process of judgmental thinking.

Forgiveness is for people, not for actions. When we are faced with an awful mistake, be it our own or someone else's, it is far more effective to forgive ourselves and/or the other person and to give the mistake over to the universe. The relinquishment of judgment invites wisdom in to handle the problem. When you forgive in this manner, watch the course of events that follow as they work in a way to rectify the mistake. Holding onto judgment simply keeps breathing life into the trauma so that we perceive it happening over and over again.

Kayleigh was given a homework assignment. She was asked to consider the events of her own past without any self-judgment. As she practiced this, she realized that she was at an Impasse in her *Spiritual Bridge* because of Vicarious

Trauma. She faced her separation anxiety rather than retreating from it through depression. She took a leap of faith and exchanged her purpose from self-abuse to connecting with her higher mind. She relinquished judgment and therefore changed her mind. As Kayleigh became more centered on mending her Spiritual Bridge, her VT symptoms diminished. She began to become less depressed, less isolated, and, not coincidentally, she met a woman at work who shared that she too had lost a child. Kayleigh helped her colleague bring the loss to closure through forgiveness and peace. Kayleigh also began strengthening her relationships with her two younger daughters, who really needed the unconditional love of an available mother. Kayleigh let herself heal and its effects extended out to heal the lives of her clients. Spiritual bridging makes healthy alliances.

When was the last time you forgave yourself for struggling in your work? When was the last time you asked for forgiveness for a mistake you made, remembering that you are worthy of forgiveness? You probably haven't done any of these recently. And we all suffer, because unforgiving behaviors have made a professional mentality that dictates that we should attack, be attacked, or avoid it all and take no risks. Fear-based thinking sets professionals up to feel ashamed of themselves when they are experiencing VT rather than to be accepting, self-compassionate, and open to seeking help.

Did you know you could be forgiven without formally saying you were sorry? Did you know that you can forgive someone who has never apologized to you? Nothing does your heart more good than to forgive yourself for some mistake, such as where you said to another, "I've acted like such a jerk. Will you forgive me?" However, certain mistakes we can no longer rectify in person. For these, we must choose to forgive ourselves.

Forgiveness is a purely reciprocal process. When you forgive yourself, the other involved is forgiven as well. Every time you forgive yourself, you see the meaning in forgiving others. When you forgive others, you are no longer attached to them through fear and shame. Collaborations in fear and shame precipitate more of the same and draw in a lot of negativity. These types of attachments imprison us in trauma symptoms and prohibit us from realizing the power of the spiritual perspective.

Justification is the obstacle to forgiveness. We think we have the right to bear a grievance based on our perceptions of client trauma. Our perceptions are points of view, not absolute truth. Justification is the misuse of the intellectual self to set up a distraction from our own fearful separation anxiety. We are so used to pain and suffering, we practically worship them. If we were to give them up, we believe there would be a huge inner void. For some, the release of pain and suffering would throw them into such an identity crisis that they think there would be nothing left at all. So, in order to sustain a false sense of security, they unconsciously uphold fear as the object of their faith by justifying their reasons to be angry at a cruel world and to withhold forgiveness. The next time you feel very upset with someone else's traumatic story, take notice of your judgmental thinking.

Sandy, a 25-year-old lawyer, came to see us very shortly after she began working as a public defender and after her parents divorced. Sandy became very depressed and highly volatile shortly after she was assigned a gruesome rape case in which the victim was a girl close to her own age.

Sandy was actually referred to us by her mother, who had been in counseling right at the time her husband left her after 27 years of marriage. Her mother had a history of depression offset by episodes of rage that were terrifying to whoever happened to be present at the time. The husband, who was having a lengthy affair with a colleague, left because he was tired of caretaking what he perceived to be a non-functioning spouse. In their years together, he was constantly walking on eggshells around his wife, being the proverbial nice guy and not rocking the boat. During all their years together, he never asked her to stop even though her acting-in and out was hurting both of them and their two children as well.

Sandy's mother was a second-born daughter and Sandy was a second-born daughter as well. Her mother fared very well in treatment and when she terminated treatment she had a home of her own, a full-time job as supervisor for a four-star resort, and a sense of peacefulness and power over her life.

Sandy's presenting problem of work-related stress unveiled her recent memory of an unfortunate turn of events when, at the age of 16, she and her partner went to a party with Sandy's older sister. There, she became very drunk and revealed to her sister that she was gay. Sandy then had a forceful argument with her partner, left the party, and hailed a cab to get her home. She started conversing with the driver and reported to him that she was gay.

After the cab passed the turn-off to her house, Sandy realized she was not going home. The driver took her to a desolate spot and raped her. Being drunk, Sandy was unable to fight him off. Sandy was in deep emotional crisis about recovering this memory at the time she came to us for counseling. The part of this presenting problem that piqued our curiosity was that after the episode, she went directly home and showered for two hours. Why would a highly intelligent girl who is an activist for feminine rights destroy important physical evidence that would directly lead to the arrest of her assailant?

The rape case Sandy was assigned was traumatizing and triggered old business for Sandy. The explanation was found once we revealed the history. In the course of growing up with Sandy's particular set of circumstances, she felt extremely frightened of her mother's behavior at a very young age. She also perceived that her father was doing virtually nothing to protect her. To distract herself from her fear, Sandy took on the protective role in the family. She spent exorbitant amounts of time being the perfect child and maintaining her mother's sanity. She would interact with her mother for hours on end in an attempt to keep her steady. This was an exercise in futility, since we can never really be in control of someone else's sanity. Sandy was repeatedly only as good as her last performance. The pressure was constantly on her to keep plugging away and so she did. Unfortunately, this was useless to her mother, who was enabled to never take responsibility for her own feelings and behaviors.

Once the divorce occurred and her mother took a turn for the better, Sandy believed she had no purpose and no identity. Behind all that, she carried a deep anger for her father and men in general, who she perceived as being very betraying and abandoning. Sandy compensated by professionally defending powerless people.

She primarily struggled with repeating "I am valueless," a judgment she made as a child who thought that if she were of any value, her father certainly would have watched over and protected her. The memory of the rape with the absence of assailant accountability sustained her unconscious re-creation of male betrayal.

The fear and shame she carried from childhood flourished in the incorrect childhood perception that in some way she deserved her paternal abandonment. She judged that she was not lovable or valuable enough to receive any better. She wasn't acceptable to her personal God and this judgment she had perpetuated on her own. After the betrayal of rape, she betrayed herself by washing away important evidence. Once again, she saw herself as a victim who was powerless and out of control.

Sandy came to quickly understand her vulnerability for Vicarious Trauma in her work. So, in our time together, she focused her attention on letting go of her past through reciprocal forgiveness. She bridged into her own perceived void and realized it was no void at all. She understood it was a place inside that was originally meant for her spiritual self, something she had abandoned through her distraction of being the perfect child.

The rape is in the past. It is now a memory like all memories, and can be rendered meaningless through forgiveness. Sandy exchanged her purpose in counseling. She relinquished self-judgment and, in so doing, corrected her trauma-based perception of the experience as a glimpse of a fear-based world in which the choices seem to be attack, be attacked, or take no risks and avoid it all. Her new purpose inspired her to extend to her Higher Mind and to others by serving as a gifted criminal lawyer. Her relationship with her parents grew closer and is steadily improving.

Releasing the past through the relinquishment of judgment begins mending the Impasse in the **Spiritual Bridge** and launches the recovery from Vicarious Trauma. Now that we have exchanged our purpose and therefore changed our minds, we are ready to use thoughts of peace to change our behaviors when we are being challenged by fear and dread through the stories we hear at work.

Responding to Fear
I Know

There is a big difference between responding and reacting when we are attending to the trauma narratives of our clients. Reacting involves little or no spiritual connection. It is ruled by the right brain or the unconscious mind and is predicated upon neural circuitry that has been rooted in some aspect of the past. To react is to act back or to act again and can become the re-creation drama of the Impasse. Reaction is defensive in nature and is based on the primitive brain's instinct of fight or flight. We react when we have a need to protect ourselves. Sometimes this is desirable. If a car is coming right at you, luckily you will react by swerving your own vehicle out of the way. In the immediacy of physically threatening situations, the fight or flight instinct kicks in automatically and is not based in hearing trauma content or on the projection of our past. Reaction skills are very useful when we find ourselves in physically dangerous circumstances.

Responding involves the introduction of a reply or an answer and is associated with the conscious left-brain. How do we answer in emotionally fearful conditions? Many of us tend to use the same fight or flight reaction in emotionally fearful circumstances. That looks like either verbally attacking the fearful subject or withdrawing from it. In emotionally scary circumstances with clients, neither of these reactive options is very useful simply because they breathe life into the fear and suffering they are attempting to eradicate. Attacking someone puts us in the perpetrator position. Withdrawing from someone puts us in the victim position. Either way, we keep ourselves stuck in the drama triangle and we feel a lot of pain.

Joan, a young nurse, 30 years old, came to see us because she was still on the fence about getting a legal divorce after a seven-month separation from her husband. Joan explained that she was feeling afraid to make a decision. Being officially on her own seemed frightening and giving her rage-filled husband the bad news seemed equally as frightening. Joan withdrew from a scary set of circumstances and the more she withdrew, the more life she breathed into her own fear.

She had already been living physically apart from her husband for seven months and she worked double shifts in the ICU to pay her living expenses. While she was able to live independently from a financial point of view, her controlling husband continued to keep track of the money and keep track of Joan. Joan never really moved through any of the emotional challenges of independent adult living because she still felt compelled to answer to her estranged husband about her life. Joan also chose not to face the unacceptability of her husband's abusive behavior. His aggressive behavior had a paralyzing effect on her and her decision to check out from it actually reinforced his tendency to go after her, once again breathing life into the very thing that scared her.

Joan shared with us that in her work she was particularly stressed about a 62-year-old female patient who was admitted after suffering a stroke. As the woman began the slow road to recovery, the woman's grown children told Joan numerous shocking stories about the woman's abusive marriage. Joan reported that she felt more depressed, inert, and unmotivated since she began caring for this patient.

Shortly after getting Joan's history, we were able to suggest to her that she was suffering from Vicarious Trauma. Our first point to her was that making no decision about being married might be, in fact, a decision. Either you are in a relationship or you are not. She thought she was avoiding a divorce. We believed she was avoiding the marriage and a decision not to be married. Her difficulty was not in her apparent ambivalence; her difficulty was her reacting rather than responding to her fear. Her reacting took the form of emotional paralysis. She was going through the motions of daily living like a robot, functioning well at completing necessary tasks, but dissociated and experiencing no joy in life. What was her fear? Her fear was of abandonment, the fear was being triggered through her work, and that fear had its roots in a much earlier time.

When Joan was 10 years old, her alcoholic, rageaholic father began to sexually molest her. This continued for about six years, as her father threatened Joan in a number of ways if she were to ever make a fuss or tell anyone. Joan was at her father's mercy for a very long time. Adding insult to injury, Joan's mother refused to believe and protect her daughter when, at 16 years old, Joan mustered up the courage to tell her the sordid tale. Joan was trained at a young age to take flight from fear. She learned to withdraw and dissociate from a fearful situation. She buried the tragic memory of her youth. She also unconsciously re-created the history in her marriage to an abusive man, held herself at his mercy, and ironically abandoned herself over and over again by not responding to her fears. The VT she suffered through her work became her emotional tipping point and was making it impossible to keep it all together through the way she had become accustomed.

After we ascertained that she no longer wanted to be married, her husband certainly escalated with inappropriate behavior. Joan commented that she was always afraid that he would react with rage. We then pointed out that her husband's abusiveness was his problem and not hers. She took on the responsibility for his problem because that was the position she took on with her father at an earlier time in her life. Joan recognized that her fear was the fear of a defenseless little girl. She had until this point judged herself as shameful and inadequate. She went undercover by becoming a miracle worker for those people on the brink of death.

When she relinquished self-judgment, she began parenting herself very differently. She stopped working double shifts. She calmly started setting very clear boundaries with her soon-to-be ex. She filed for divorce, opened her own bank and charge accounts, and served her spouse with an order of protection. With each responsive step she took toward emotional freedom, her fear shrank respectively. She reported a sense of peacefulness about herself and her ex as she let go. She began to build confidence and started to have faith in her abilities. The burden of VT transformed into a blessing, as it offered Joan a powerful opportunity to heal.

Responding to fear sustains our release of the past. Once we have relinquished the self-judgment unconsciously made in a much earlier time, we need to stay peaceful when we meet up with a scary present work situation that triggers our primitive brain. When we commit to letting go of the past by becoming conscious of it, we state "I can," which affirms our decision to no longer perceive ourselves as victims. When fear is triggered through the trauma content we hear at work, we can now state that we know what is really going on. We are right at the Impasse and now know what to do so that we do not turn back. We meet and rise above separation anxiety, as we remember that we are not abandoned, not alone, and are worthy of our Higher Mind's protective love. Responding rather than reacting implies thinking peacefully or calmly when we are deciding what to do or what to say in a scary situation.

Emotional reacting occurs as a result of poor impulse control. It has been found that the brain's frontal lobes, usually regarded as the set of higher order functions, forge powerful connections to the limbic system of the primitive brain. When fear is triggered, our immediate gut impulse is to get away from the feeling because it is so unpleasant. So we impulsively turn to distracting behaviors that ultimately only serve to give fear reign over our lives. We abandon ourselves in the process by dishonoring what it is we are feeling. Ironically, the distracting behaviors tend to get out of control and help us to believe that we are incompetent at functioning in the world. Acknowledging fear is required in order to respond to it in a healthy way.

We started working with Leila, a 40-year-old female attorney, very "successful" in her career and very unsuccessful in a 14-year-long collaboration in fear she called marriage. Her husband, struggling with his own avoidance of fear, moved out after he told her he was sick and tired of putting up with her rage and intense verbal attacks. Leila was shocked at Jim's "impulsive behavior" of leaving, which she described as extreme. When she started counseling, she insisted that Jim was experiencing midlife crisis. She wanted to spend her therapeutic dollar talking about how troubled he had always been and how she continually rescued him in their time together. She represented that she was not an attacking person and, clearly, Jim did not appreciate how hard she had worked to make sure he was happy.

Leila was an adoption attorney. She made a lot of money in this field, but it cost her dearly in her emotional well-being. In the process of arranging adoptions, Leila would hear some very tragic stories around the circumstances of any particular baby's biological family of origin. Leila was overtly stoic about these devastating stories, but they were clearly taking their toll on her.

The first three weeks of our relationship, Leila would call us every other day. Usually clients call between appointments when they are in some type of emotional crisis. Whenever we returned those early calls, Leila would not tell us she was in crisis, she would act it out.... right in our direction. One time she called and asserted that she needed to talk to one of us right away. When we returned her call, she did not answer the phone. On the third try she was there and her question was, "Jim invited me to dinner tonight. Should I go?" She was reminded that she had called; the assumption was that she was in crisis. If she was feeling fearful about something, she needed to talk about that. Another time, she left two voice mails wanting to speak with one of us and upon our return call pointedly asked, "Did Jim call you?" Our response: "Why not ask Jim directly?" We reiterated that when she called between sessions for help, she needed to be in touch with her feelings of terror and talk about that.

Soon thereafter, Leila left a message on our voice mail canceling all further appointments. When we called her back, she stated with remarkable hostility that she needed "shrinks who would be more soothing and comforting" to her. After one or two information questions, she revealed that she had a very difficult weekend and she was afraid to call for help. Leila was ashamed and afraid to have and express her fear. After all, she was an all-powerful lawyer who performed miracles for people. She couldn't possibly need help in any way. Her impulse upon fear was to distract herself by going after people on a superficial level to make herself feel better. This was fruitless because, at these times, she would withhold what it was she was really feeling anyway. Instead, she would behave in a pushy manner, which pushed people away. Moreover, her reaction to fear by getting aggressive got her the opposite of what she said she wanted: comfort.

Jim was at the end of the line with being on the receiving end of unkind treatment, and quite frankly so were we. When we explained to Leila what we observed about her behavior, we concluded by stating that we believed she was suffering from Vicarious Trauma. We believed she needed to look into that directly and if that didn't resonate for her, we would be happy to refer her out for a better fit. We were very clear that we did not want to enable her in the continuing dance around her issues. At that point in our conversation, she emphatically had a change of heart and wanted an extra session that week.

Vicarious Trauma took its toll on Leila in that she was re-creating some painful scenario from her past and the outcome appeared to be abandonment. Now that Leila was ready to get down to work, she revealed that she was raised as an only child in the swank Park Avenue section of New York City. Her father was a busy doctor who was rarely home. Her mother was a very beautiful and very depressed former model who was overmedicating herself with a lot of prescription drugs. Even though she was there physically, she really wasn't there emotionally. Leila was passed off to a series of nannies. One day her mother took it too far and died from a prescription medicine overdose. Leila's father never really dealt with the tragedy and indulged Leila to try to keep her happy. Leila shared that her favorite pastime as a child was reading the Little Madeline books, which was a series about a French orphan.

Leila's work was now traumatizing her by triggering an historical event for which the legitimate grief was deferred. Leila needed to have that grief, but she felt afraid and out of control when it came to the surface of her consciousness. She lost her mother, was abandoned and that terrible event needed to be honored.

What she would come to know in her recovery was that the abandonment drama was always initiated with her own self-abandonment by dishonoring her feeling state when it was fear. Fear and subsequent self-abandonment is always the backdrop for re-creation of the Impasse.

Responding rather than reacting to emotional fear is the most important part of recovering from Vicarious Trauma. Responding is a discipline and it requires much mental structure and practice in order to become efficient at it. Responding to fear is best developed by following three distinct behavioral steps: *STOP, LOOK,* and *LISTEN!* Do you remember this phrase being taught to you as a child when you were learning how to cross the street? It is a fitting analogy. Some streets are easier to cross than others. How many streets have you crossed when you never even bothered to *Stop, Look, and Listen?* At some of the dangerous intersections, you could easily be mowed down if you didn't adhere to the rule. When you find yourself at a scary emotional intersection in your work, the rule of responding is to *Stop, Look, and Listen.*

Let's start with *Stop.* Identify your personal red light. For some of us, our anger is our personal red light. When we feel afraid due to some trauma content we have heard on the job, our acting-out distraction from the feeling of fear may be to become angry. Perhaps something is going on in the client's story that is triggering an historical fear or an early break to our spiritual perspective. We might typically become impatient, frustrated, irritated, and angry. That is our red light. STOP! We are at a gap in the *Spiritual Bridge*, an Impasse. Don't retreat back into the darkness of the ego and breathe more life into the fear.

Simply *STOP.* Also be humble and realistic by sharing that sometimes we will stop sooner than others, as those close to us will be happy to attest. But with practice we become better and better at stopping sooner, which is a much nicer way to treat ourselves.

Untreated Vicarious Trauma sets us up to distract ourselves from historical fear with various acting-in or acting-out behaviors. In these situations, we are invariably the ones who suffer most. Ironically, when the acting-out distraction is anger, we can find ourselves at a place where the problem of getting mad becomes the greatest reminder of our need to respond rather than react.

It doesn't take long to identify a personal stop light. Just make sure you never tell yourself "I don't know" or "I'm trying" as you begin to develop this skill. The statements "I don't know" and "I'm trying" are two of the most popular distractions to avoid dealing with fear. These two statements are a profound form of self-abandonment that keeps us stuck in the victim position, widens the Impasse, and leaves the individual feeling powerless and hopeless. There is really no such thing as trying when we make choices for dealing with trauma. We are either doing it or not doing it. We don't have to be hard on ourselves when we are not doing it, but let's at least be honest about it. Being honest with ourselves unblocks the path of forward movement. When we ask ourselves the hard questions about our acting-in or acting-out distractions, the answer "I don't know" is only more denial of Vicarious Trauma and is feeding into our struggle with the underlying theme of incompetence. It undermines our ability to respond to fear. Of course we know why, but if we copped to it we'd then take on the responsibility of being human like everyone else.

If you are afraid to look at "why," simply say so as a first step in rising above fear. Stop and honor your feeling of fear. It is okay and it makes perfect sense that you would experience fear in working with populations that tell appalling stories.

We always know in our heart of hearts what's going on with us. Stuck in the ego, we tend to be afraid to *LOOK* at it. When we stop the distracting behaviors, we free ourselves to look inward and reveal the truth in what is happening. We are suffering from VT. We can then *LISTEN* peacefully to our inner story and realize we deserve to relinquish judgment; to be more patient with ourselves and the traumatizing aspects of our work. The *LISTEN* part is where we allow a thought of peace to enter our minds.

The enigma is that many of us try to overcome fear out of our egos, a system based in fear to begin with. For example, we might get very intellectual in our attempt to overcome fear. We go to conferences, take continuing education, preserve our credentials, and keep current on our malpractice insurance. We have a wealth of education and information, but consistently tend to not integrate the information in a way that affords us the opportunity to recognize our own level of work-related stress.

Another example: we focus physically. We work out regularly at the gym, become nutrition enthusiasts, and take yoga and kick boxing. Yet we still do not feel sound.

Another pattern: we tout the importance of emotional growth and spend exorbitant amounts of time with others so that they might become whole, while we do nothing about our own emotional well-being.

When we cannot integrate what we know to be true into what we believe to be true, we are at that familiar Impasse in the Spiritual Bridge and suffering from our own trauma reaction. When we consciously exchange our purpose from maintaining ourselves at the Impasse to bridging to our higher consciousness, we can acknowledge our fear and separation anxiety because we are then empowered to do something about it. We can meet discouraging feeling states because we know what to do when we are in them. We give the feelings to our higher brain and receive peace in return. Spiritual training can actually raise the baseline happiness set point of the brain. It can change the basic pattern of prefrontal activation in a way that elicits more positive emotion. This inner transition is then environmentally mirrored for us through a series of corrective and uplifting events.

Responding to fear is the exercise of free will for freedom from Vicarious Trauma; freedom from absorbing the pain and suffering our clients' stories tend to impose on themselves, and vicariously, on us. Responding, rather than reacting, brings with it the knowledge of our true higher purpose—to extend and receive love. Once we know our purpose, we are ready to link up to our higher brain. We are worthy and therefore ready to receive and offer love freely. Through this reciprocal process, we perceive ourselves to be centered in the **present**. Here we heal from trauma and experience peace, creativity, and joy.

Reconnecting to the Spirit
I AM

Reconnecting to the Spirit is receiving the power of the higher mind. This is the moment of truth. Now you are ready to be who you truly are. Once you have moved through the first four steps you are ready to complete the exchange. You have relinquished judgment of yourself. You have used thoughts of peace to let go of fear. You are now ready to move from the neural circuitry that runs through your primitive brain to receive your higher Self. This is the only step that mentally requires you to do absolutely nothing. Just be still. Simply be present for the *Higher Mind*. Mending the *Spiritual Bridge* has opened the way.

No longer invested in maintaining the false idols of historical grievances continually reinforced through VT and having moved beyond separation anxiety, you are ready to receive the characteristics of the *Spiritual Self*. This requires no concerted effort on your part. It is the accepting portion of the exchange of purpose. These characteristics come naturally as you reconnect. At this point, it is important to remember that a state of readiness to receive them is not the same as a state of mastery in receiving them. Readiness is the decision to receive these qualities as precious gifts delivered from our higher mind. Mastery is embracing the attributes so that they become the core of your identity, which had become so disjointed through trauma. Repetition and practice in accepting these traits brings us to mastery of them. Readiness occurs as you remember your true identity—a good human, sometimes spiritually referred to as the *I Am*.

Reconnecting to the Spirit implies release of the past and response to fear or the application of self-forgiveness. When we have exercised this enough times, forgiveness tends to come to mind quickly and doesn't require much concerted effort. Think about how much psychic energy we pour into fear-based distractions, within ourselves and with others. If we gave a fraction of that energy to the discipline of connecting to the higher brain, our state of mind and our interactions would be far more centered and peaceful.

Those who spend little or no time in bridging to the higher mind tend to complain that they have difficulty in relating to some personal concept of a Higher Power. No wonder! They exert little or no energy in that inner relationship and are then disappointed about it. "God" doesn't travel the Drama Triangle. We are not victims waiting to be rescued by a bearded old man in the sky. Furthermore, why do we receive something so great so infrequently? It makes sense that with the chronic stress in our jobs compared to what we get in bridging, we would be bridging all the time. Bridging to the *I Am* or building a relationship with the Spiritual Self needs our input. M. Scott Peck wrote in *The Road Less Traveled* that in building a loving relationship, many times quantity is quality time. Devote some time to your Spiritual Self. You are worthy of it.

How you practice mastery in reconnecting is a very personal and individual-ized practice. You will create bridging exercises that work for you. Religion, or a particular style of expressing faith in a Higher Power, is only one form of practicing mastery.

We have gathered a partial list of bridging exercises that may help you create your own path.

- Meditate.
- Practice yoga.
- Be in nature.
- Engage in the arts.
- Pray for someone.
- Read and journal.
- Cook a meal for someone.
- Stargaze.
- Help the sick.
- Attend someone else's church or temple.
- Exercise.
- Perform charitable acts.
- Take care of children.
- Play games.
- Help the elderly.
- Teach.
- Read for the blind.
- Participate in an ecological endeavor.
- Join or form a spiritual study or encouragement group.
- Give compliments.
- Listen actively.
- Pay attention.
- Express gratitude.
- Be present.

When we are peaceful in our minds, we receive the energy of the *I Am*. This energy gives us the characteristics of trust, honesty, tolerance, gentleness, joy, self-intimacy, generosity, patience, faithfulness, and open-mindedness. First, we utilize these characteristics unto ourselves. This feels so wonderfully liberating and powerful that we are enthusiastic to extend the same to others. We then co-create spiritual alliances.

Trust is the first characteristic we receive as we let our minds be still. Having moved through the first four steps, we have trust in ourselves as we remove the Under Construction sign that earlier stood at the Impasse. We can let go of the illusion of control and self-judgment that kept us in denial about our own legitimate work-related misery. Our minds are peaceful and we trust that is all that is necessary to receive the healing power of the Spiritual Perspective.

Self-honesty is the essence of the *I Am*. Honesty can be described as consistency. It signifies the elimination of inner conflict due to what was once a need to distract ourselves from the affliction of trauma. It marks the end of self-deception or denial. It proclaims our self-acceptance and opens the way back to our true identities. Reconnecting to the higher mind also keeps us honest with ourselves when we are tempted to stray off the path of recovery. It is the motivation that reminds us to remember the first four steps when we meet up with separation anxiety.

Self-tolerance is the result of the relinquishment of self-judgment. We now understand that we are not perfect, we can not compete with "God" by performing miracles and we are human just like everyone else. Honesty helps us notice that we will make errors and that going into shame about it only furthers our trauma. Self-tolerance protects us from going into that shame attack when we have made a mistake. Noticing that an error has been made now comes from an unspoiled awareness, not from a position of judgment and fear. Free of shame, we can give the error over to our higher brain and thereby invite wisdom in to handle the problem. Tolerance helps us remember that we are worthy to receive a personal sense of Higher Power because we are not separate. Therefore, we maintain a position of being self-accepting and letting infinite wisdom resolve the daily challenges of hearing trauma content through our work.

Gentleness can be described as the inability to do harm to oneself or anyone else. When we live gently with ourselves, we make a conscious decision to not berate ourselves for our professional or personal struggles. Berating oneself furthers the negative force of any trauma narrative. Self-harm is only an issue when one is invested in holding onto judgment as a way to stay separate and be "true" to an insane belief that we are not worthy of connecting to our Higher Self or Higher Consciousness. Gentleness is strength and spiritually and does not imply the worldly connotation of passivity or numbness.

Joy is the awareness and appreciation of the goodness and the beauty in you, something we are highly at risk to lose sight of when we suffer from VT. It is the state we achieve when we are honest, tolerant, and gentle. Joy is different from the feeling called "glad" or "happy." Happy is a feeling that results from happenstance or some pleasing outside event. Joy is the resulting state of the most precious inside event. It is a state of release that is free of fear, shame, and anger. As we receive joy, we begin to pay attention to our wonder rather than our woe. When we have met and risen above our separation anxiety, joy is what we experience in its place. It is a very powerful place to be.

Self-intimacy is experienced as a result of defenselessness. With fear nullified, our defenses no longer serve a purpose. We are free of the need to protect ourselves from the context of a painful past, set up again and again through listening to the trauma stories of others. Defensiveness is what kept our VT symptoms as the altars at which we worshiped. As we receive intimacy, we state, "I could find out nothing about myself that would make me unlovable to my Higher Consiousness." Self-intimacy is the characteristic that compels us to extend love to others. It is the mainstay of a spiritual alliance and is so important in helping others heal.

Generosity with ourselves is received as we reconnect. This is not the fear-based characteristic of greed. Greed is the fear-based result of being separated from our Higher Selves. Greed is a distraction based in thoughts of lack and scarcity. When we are separate, perceiving ourselves as alone, we believe we have nothing and so compensate by keeping things for ourselves. Generosity with oneself signifies the quality of quantity time connecting to the higher mind. Being generous with ourselves means receiving the abundance of peace in us as much as we can. Ironically, when this generosity is received we are driven to give it away to others. Generosity is the main dynamic that ensures we stay the path of spiritual connection.

Patience with ourselves is received in the *I Am*. Since being in the present is the human experience of eternity, there are no time constraints and therefore no need for impatience. No longer separate, we release the need to control things based on being the only person to do the job. Since we give away control based in fear, we gain patience within and set healthier boundaries for ourselves and with others. Passion is the root word of patience and we begin to feel that passion again in our work. Patience gives us clear inner vision. When we use inner vision to perceive any particular event, we have faith that the event serves us by either protecting us or providing us with some new self-understanding. We have faith that we will be spiritually served by the event, even if it doesn't appear that way in its original traumatizing manifestation.

Open-mindedness occurs as we receive the power of the higher mind and, with it, are empowered to take risks, extend ourselves, and realize the talents and abilities we possess on a grand scale. We begin to see with a vision that is not of our eyes and to believe that there are no limits to the possibilities. As we accept this vision for ourselves, we see the endless possibilities for others. Creativity soars, enthusiasm resounds, and courage abounds. It is the open mind that has the power to view healing as an event that occurs, but never from an ego-driven need to control.

It is important to differentiate between embracing these characteristics and acting them out. There are some who get into what we call a case of the tail wagging the dog. They think that if they act patient, tolerant, and so on, then that will be acceptable. This is not how it works. When we are out of denial about our own trauma reactions, in release of the past and responding to fear, we are centered in the present and able to receive these spiritual gifts. We do not act them out, we become them.

When work's traumatizing challenges harm us, impair us, or trigger our historical upsets, we can remember forgiveness (relinquishment of judgment followed with a thought of peace) quite easily with a mended Spiritual Bridge. Connection to the higher mind or the spiritual perspective empowers us to stay centered and trustworthy of our ability to cope with the certainty of Vicarious Trauma we experience through helping others.

Chapter Eight: Organizations as Vicarious Trauma Cauldrons

As we gathered stories and testimonials from helping professionals during the creation of this book, one common theme became obvious and that is that helping professionals are terrified to discuss their trauma. The only way they were willing to share their stories with us was with our promise to maintain their anonymity. In a survey conducted by Wilson and Thomas, over 79.9% of surveyed helpers reported having difficulty discussing their exposure to Vicarious Trauma, 75% felt alienated from their peers, 73% felt a lack of support from their licensing boards and professional organizations, and over 62% felt reluctant to speak honestly about Vicarious Trauma at all (Wilson & Thomas, 2004).

When professionals were asked why they believe they are susceptible to VT, these were their responses, as cited in the 1998 Second Annual Poster Session for organizational coping strategies:

- lack of experience with trauma victims;
- case loads too high with trauma victims;
- hearing repetitive stories of trauma or abuse;
- working with clients who re-enact pathological relationships in therapy or in the helping relationship itself;
- working without adequate support or supervision;
- fear of asking for help due to being seen as incompetent;
- experiencing a traumatic event with a client, such as an attempted suicide or a suicide or other severe psychiatric break from reality;
- working with clients in a work context in which concrete signs of success are few;
- empathizing with client's experiences of severe pain in their lives and not being able to hold to strong boundaries;
- unable to maintain a professional distance consistent with the ethical standards outlined by professional boards (McSwain, Robinson, & Panteluk, 1998).

One therapist reported the following incident that remains with her to this day:

I was seeing a client who admitted he had a serious addiction to prescription drugs and had committed to go for treatment. His consumption was so profuse that I had no idea how he drove a car or functioned in his high-level professional career. One day, he came for therapy and brought his 7-year-old daughter, who waited in my waiting room. How he drove to my office that day with his daughter in the car was appalling to me. During the session it became apparent that he was highly debilitated and, as he spoke, he began to lose consciousness. I was in a serious dilemma: his child was in the waiting room, counting on her father to take her to ballet following the session.

The father was, in effect, passed out on my couch, and unable to function at even the most minimal level, let alone drive this child in a car. It was obvious that another adult had to be called to assist with this situation. Yet, the child would be certainly be traumatized when another adult or emergency vehicle arrived to take care of her father in this extremely diminished capacity. As I quickly made a professional decision to call an emergency responder, I had to compress my own trauma response, make emergency decisions for an incapacitated person where the liability could potentially have been overwhelming, and then provide guidance and support for his young child who was not my client and appeared to be in a state of absolute panic as I approached her in the waiting room.
Janine, Clinical Social Worker

Another therapist wrote the following:

Although I worked in an office with three other therapists, we were individual practitioners and so had very little professional interaction in the course of a work day. Never before did I feel the estrangement from my peers than when I had an overwhelming event take place in my office. A client came to see me for an intake session. She had been released two days prior from an in-patient program. She filled out her forms and began to share with me her path of recovery from a lifetime from physical and sexual abuse. When I asked her about medication, she recited a laundry list of ingredients that made up one heck of a psychotropic cocktail. As she began to share her history, her eyes rolled back into her head, and she stiffened up in the chair. I called her name three or four times before I realized that this client had gone catatonic before my eyes. No amount of talking, calling, or even raising my voice could move her from this paralyzed state. I went to the intake form and called the emergency number. It was a non-working number.

I ran to offices of my peers, knocked on two of three office doors, asking for some help and some guidance. Instead, I received an absolute resistance to become involved. In fact, the best response I got was a blank stare from someone with whom I had worked for many years. Feeling helpless, inadequate, and at fault, I finally dialed 9-1-1. What really struck me as dysfunctional was my numbing to the point that much of my concern was around keeping my next client waiting.
Donald, Psychologist

We must be able to identify Vicarious Traumatization without shame or fear of reprisal. As professionals, we need to recognize that VT is a veritable occupational hazard. We must accept helpers' reactions as expected and normal responses and provide a safe environment for debriefing and healing.

Over time, if we have not adapted to the trauma stories we have heard, our entire psychological, biological, and spiritual system begins to wear down and malfunction. You will recognize system failure when you are inadequately responding to the trauma content. We need to be aware of the length, duration, and intensity of our exposure, the type of clients involved, especially if they are suicidal or children, and our own trauma histories. Additionally, organizational factors worsen VT by overworking staff and providing insufficient staffing, supervision, and consultation. This needs to be addressed immediately so that those in the helping professions can continue to provide a much-needed service to the community.

In order to prevent VT, organizations can advocate for the continued strength of the stated ethical principles and guidelines of their professions for their licensees, group members, employees and staff through social support, group cohesion, training, and trauma-informed staffing supervision and consultation (McSwain et al., 1998). Setting a hierarchical structure from the ranks of the leaders in authority to the workers carrying out the tasks in the field, the awareness of VT as a problem that needs to be solved is our goal. From the Board level to the management level and to the working level, ensuring that all are informed. The risks of not addressing this silent killer could lead to a community of traumatized helpers. Everyone must be encouraged to address this problem so they can maintain the strong ethical principles of autonomy, beneficence, non-malfeasance, and justice. If left untreated, VT can become emotionally contagious, with numbing, hypervigilance, irritability, indifference, cynicism, hopelessness, and despair spreading rampant amongst the ranks.

Appropriate staff or professional training for the prevention of VT includes the following essential pieces:

• recognition that VT is in fact an occupational hazard and is destigmatized within the organization or practice group;
• honoring and respecting one another as human beings as well as helping professionals;
• supporting wellness by providing adequate vacation time, sick time, and personal leave;
• building a culture of excellence;
• providing adequate pay and benefits;
• rewarding clinical skills;
• setting positive goals;
• building up buffering strategies;
• always backing up your team;
• creating a safe learning community and encouraging and rewarding continuing education;
• obtaining consultation for yourselves as administrators, managers, and supervisors;
• being confidential and never penalizing someone for revealing VT;
• training competent supervisors who understand the dynamics of VT; and
• requiring supervision to prevent the contagion that VT can perpetrate upon a healthy organization (International Trauma Consultants, 2006);
• organizations need to provide adequate supervision for the critical helping structure inherent in every healing relationship that includes:
    ~ a safe, nurturing environment with clear and appropriate role bound aries in which the client's affect and the helper's empathic strain are both successfully and individually managed;
    ~ conscious attention paid to the nonverbal piece of the relationship, the right brain reaction, such as feelings, memories, and autonomic body responses such as increased heart and breathing rate so that helpers can be aware of and effectively manage the reaction they are experiencing;

~ heightened awareness of the levels of countertransference that are occurring must be taken into account (i.e., the client and helper countertransference, the helper and the administrative body countertransference, the colleague to colleague countertransference, and the helper to the licensing board or governing body countertransference);

• maintaining components of VT supervision: awareness of VT as a real problem, theoretical understanding of VT, an understanding of childhood development, an ability to focus on the conscious and unconscious aspects of the helping relationship, creating a safe, private, and confidential interpersonal climate with helpers so they can process their VT without shame or fear of judgment, being educated in VT and attuned to the helper's condition or state (Wilson & Lindy, 2004).

A helping organization that pays strict attention to the prevention and healing of Vicarious Trauma will glean positive results. These results will include healthy transformation of the client, healthy transformation of the helper as a professional and healthy transformation of the helping professional as a person. If the organization is doing its job, then this is the ultimate result.

Following is a cogent case study presented by Doug, a psychologist / custody evaluator. Doug functioned in a therapeutic private practice in addition to performing custody evaluations for the court in litigated divorce cases. In his jurisdiction, custody cases were either assigned by the judge in the family court or Doug was selected by the divorcing couple and his appointment agreed to by stipulation of the divorcing parties to perform these custody evaluations.

I have a very active private practice and was invited by several attorneys and judges I knew to participate in the custody evaluator program in my state. To qualify, I took all the necessary training to become eligible through the court system to perform custody evaluations. In my private practice I focused my expertise on divorcing couples and children of divorce. I also enjoyed working with stepfamilies and blended families, and believed I had the expertise to work within the scope of family law.

The court system was overloaded with divorce cases requiring custody evaluations and so I was busy as soon as I was added to the list of evaluators. The case I most remember that caused me the most anxiety involved two teenaged girls, an undiagnosed bipolar mother, and a passive but caring father. It was not my job to diagnose either party, but to determine where the children's best interests would be served in their living arrangements. I followed the protocols to the letter. I interviewed both parents and all collaterals. I had the children seen by an independent neutral child specialist, selected by the parents, so I had additional information with which to make my recommendations.

The mother was actually a very sad case. She so wanted to function as a good parent, but was emotionally out of control and was psychologically injurious to her children with her mood swings that included outbursts of rage. The father was unsophisticated and worked a blue-collar job while making every possible effort to meet the needs of two adolescent girls and their sports schedules. The mother disappeared for weeks at a time and the girls were definitive in wanting supervised visits with Mom. The majority of custodial time with Dad was assessed as appropriate. One afternoon, I received 13 angry and hysterical phone calls from Mom threatening to sue me and file a complaint with my board if I did not provide her equal access to the children. All these calls were documented.

The recommendation was made to the court to place the girls with their father and to provide supervised visitation for the mother. The recommendation was adopted by the court.

Several weeks passed with no harassing phone calls or further contact with this family. I was working way too hard, in excess of 60 hours a week, with a huge caseload of custody evaluations. Two months later, I received a Board complaint from the mom. She alleged that I was prejudiced against her, that I did not follow the protocols, that I did not interview her family, and that the child specialist selected in the case was a personal friend of mine who I influenced to select her ex-husband as primary custodian. I was freaked out for two years, until this came before the Board. I went through my files, line by line, searching for anything that could lead to such an upsetting turn in the road. I found nothing. I sent all my records to the Board and waited. After six months I contacted a representative of my licensing Board to see how the case was progressing and if they needed anything further from me. I was passed from person to person on the phone, each interaction proving fruitless in the way of getting any help. The only information I could get was that they were behind in addressing Board complaints and would get back to me.

The complaint itself was not as traumatizing as the treatment I received from my Board. There was no one there willing to assist me either with procedure or with information regarding the case. Another year went by and finally I received notice of a hearing. Once again, I contacted my board to find out what I could expect. Did I need to call witnesses? Did I need an attorney to represent me? Was my accuser being represented by counsel? Was the Board going to protect my flawless record? No response at all! They used and abused me and, when I needed them, they abandoned me. I hired an attorney to attend the hearing with me and within minutes the charges were dismissed. It was also traumatizing and heartbreaking to see the mom in so much pain and so disturbed as she acted out at the hearing. It was obvious that she suffered from mental illness.

But what was more disturbing was the lack of interaction, or support, or connection from the Board. I thought that that was my board and I was astounded at the lack of compassion about my set of circumstances. I eventually withdrew from the court roster and now only practice in a more collaborative model. As an aside, four years later, the mom called to apologize for filing the complaint to the board. She had finally sought treatment for her bipolar disorder and was now on appropriate medication. She realized that the decisions made at the time were, in fact, in the best interest of her children.

Doug, Custodial Evaluator

Helpers who work in organizational settings need to be able to talk about their feelings with colleagues who will not judge them. Organizations need to support their staff in the practice of effective interoffice communication skills that help workers communicate with people at every level of the organization. It must be remembered that, in many of these settings, caring for traumatized clients is a regular event, not an occasional occurrence. Therefore, exposure to trauma is frequent. Organizations need to offer balancing activities to their staff, which includes honoring each other as heroes who do some of the hardest and most important work for people in the world.

It is noteworthy that many ethical codes do not mention the welfare of their professional members when discussing burnout or Vicarious Traumatization. Quite the contrary! The welfare of helpers for their own sake is increasing in ethical importance. "Self-care" implies that the individual is responsible for preventing the problem and that it is the helper's problem when it does occur.

There is only so much one can achieve without a shift in the environment in which one operates. Professional organizations need to move to make an effort to support the professionals in their battle against VT. The helping professions need to expand their views to include professional welfare as an integral aspect of professional standards. This approach maintains and strengthens the clear and good judgment of the client. The client is well served, but not at the expense or sacrifice of the helper.

CONCLUSION

If you are wondering at this point if you are suffering from Vicarious Trauma— good! We've accomplished our goal. Suffering in silence only makes the situation worse and reinforces the unhealthy shame that is associated with this normal stress response. We hope that you understand that Vicarious Trauma not only affects your mind; it literally alters the structure of your brain in a counterproductive fashion. It takes time and patience to repair the damage and it takes courage to examine yourself introspectively.

We encourage you to reach out to others who, by virtue of reading this book, you know are suffering. It is so important for helpers to rally together to destigmatize the inevitability of Vicarious Trauma. Now is your opportunity to consider the Miracle Worker Reverie, detach from it, and give yourself permission to ask for help.

By reading this book, we hope you have been enlightened and have opened an important door for the helping professions. The Second - Hand Shock™ Workbook will further you on this important journey through various contemplative and interactive exercises.

We encourage you to form VT groups for collegiality, discussion, and workbook guidance. Look to create a safe haven for yourself and your colleagues. The call to help others is precious. You can preserve the integrity of the helping relationship by taking excellent care of yourself. We wish you well on your journey.

Professional Group Discussion Questions

Following are some questions from The Second - Hand Shock Workbook™. These questions are meant to generate meaningful discussion and to enhance comfort levels in dialoging about Vicarious Trauma.

1. What happens to our population if our helpers don't get treatment for VT?

2. How can consumers recognize VT symptoms in a professional they hire and what should they do?

3. How do we tell a colleague that we think he or she has VT?

4. How do we recognize our own VT?

5. What is the first step we need to take to help solve this problem?

6. How are our personal relationships affected by our VT?

7. What are we afraid of?

8. If there was one thing we could do for ourselves to combat this problem, what would it be?

9. If we were at the board level or the managing partner of a law firm, what would we do with this knowledge after reading this book?

10. As consumers, how can we support our helpers in the battle against VT?

11. Are the physical manifestations of VT reversible?

12. As a professional, what do you do about the ethical violations you know you've made because you were suffering with VT? How do you make amends?

13. Where does a professional go to receive treatment for VT?

Call the *Vicarious Trauma Institute* at *480-991-4119* for information about treatment options, which include individual weekly consultation, a three-day intensive treatment program, or a one day in-service for your organization.

Ellie and Vickie can also be contacted by email at:

Ellie Izzo   info@vicarioustrauma.com

Vicki Carpel Miller   info@vicarioustrauma.com

REFERENCES

Baldwin, D. (2007). About trauma. Retrieved May 28, 2007, from http://www.trauma_pages.com/trauma

Begley, S. (2007). Train your mind, change your brain. New York: Ballantine.

Berne, E. (1964). The games people play. New York: Ballantine.

Carll, E. (2006). Trauma psychology: The evolution of a specialty. Retrieved February 28, 2007, from the APA website: http://www.division42.org

Earley, J. (2006). Transference and countertransference. Retrieved June 8, 2007, from http://www.earley.org./Patterns/transference_and_countertransfer.htm

Fox, R., & Carey, L. (1999, Summer). Therapists' collusion with the resistance of rape survivors. Clinical Social Work Journal, 185-201.

Healing Resources Info. (2005). Santa Barbara Graduate Institute for Clinical Studies and Research. Retrieved May 28, 2004, from http://www.traumaresources.org

International Trauma Consultants. (2006). Retrieved March 6, 2007, from http://www.traumaconsultants.net

Jaffe, J., Segal, J., & Dumke, L. (2005). Emotional and psychological trauma. Retrieved February 2, 2007, from http://www.helpguide.org

Joseph, R. (1999, August 23). The neurology of traumatic 'dissociative' amnesia: Commentary and literature review. Child Abuse and Neglect, 8, 715-727.

Izzo, Ellie (2007). *The Bridge To I Am*. New York: iUniverse.

Kramer, P. (2007). Empathy: The infinite mind. Retrieved (needs date), from http://www.kmedia.com

Kennedy, E. & Charles, S. On becoming a counselor: A basic guide for non-professional counselors. New York: Crossroads.

Lee, David. (2006). The hidden costs of trauma in the workplace. Retrieved March 6, 2007, from http://www.humannatureatwork.com/workplacestress

Liberzon, I., Taylor, S., Amdur, R., Jung, T., Chamberlin, K, Minoshima, S. et al. (1999). Brain activation in PTSD in response to trauma related stimuli. Biological Psychiatry, 45(7), 817-826.

McSwain, K., Robinson, R., & Panteluk, L. (1998). Implications for practice: Therapeutic, personal, and organizational coping strategies. Retrieved May 28, 2007, from http://www.dr.jontry.com

Pearlman, L., & MacIan, P. (1995). An empirical study of the effects of trauma on work with trauma therapists. Professional Psychology: Research and Practice, 26(6), 558-565.

Pearlman, L., & Saakvitne, K. (1995). Treating therapists and vicarious traumatization and secondary traumatic stress disorders. In C. R. Figley (Ed.), Compassion fatigue: Coping with secondary traumatic stress disorder in those who treat the traumatized (Psychosocial Stress Series) (pp. 150-177). New York: Brunner Mazel.

Saakvitne, K., & Pearlman, L. (1996). Transforming the pain: A workbook on Vicarious Trauma. New York: Norton.

Santy, P. (2007). Feeling, countertransference, and reality. Retrieved June 8, 2007, from http://www.blog.spot.com/2006

Schore, A. (2003). Advances in neuropsychoanalysis attachment theory and trauma research. Psychoanalytic Inquiry, 22, 433-484.

Weingarten, K. (2003). Common shock. Witnessing violence every day: How we are harmed, how we can heal. New York: Dutton.

Weingarten, K. (2004, February). Common shock: Witnessing violence in clients' lives [Adaptation]. Counselor Magazine, 70-74.

Wilson, J., & Lindy, J. (1994). Countertransference in the treatment of PTSD. New York: Guilford Press.

Wilson, J., & Thomas, R. (2004). Empathy and the treatment of trauma and PTSD. New York: Brunner Mazel.

Part Two

The Second - Hand Shock™ Workbook

The Rapid Advance Process outlined in this workbook for addressing Vicarious Trauma is in no way a substitute for ongoing medical or psychiatric consultation, medication, individual, family, marital, or group therapy, counseling, or any other form of treatment for emotional disorders. We strongly urge our readers to seek out professional consultation for the treatment of their Vicarious Trauma.

Chapter 1: Introduction to The Second - Hand Shock™ Workbook

Notes

We have been in the helping professions collectively for over 50 years. We have suffered and seen colleagues suffer from the effects of untreated Vicarious Trauma. Unfortunately, most of us believe we have to suffer in silence. Only recently has it become a little bit more acceptable to admit we may be compromised due to the stresses of our work. *DAY AFTER DAY THE PRICE YOU PAY: Managing Your Second - Hand Shock*™ and *The Second - Hand Shock*™ *Workbook* have been created to acknowledge and address this underreported professional epidemic in a respectful, compassionate and accepting manner. We want to bring what has been considered a secretive and highly sensitive subject out in the open so those in the helping professions can secure the support, regard and assistance they so profoundly deserve. The price the helper pays, if Vicarious Trauma is left untreated, is excessive.

What is Vicarious Trauma? The technical definition of Vicarious Trauma is: a transformation in the helper's inner sense of identity and existence that results from utilizing controlled empathy when listening to clients' traumatic stories. More simply put, Vicarious Trauma is a set of cognitive, emotional, physical and spiritual disturbances that result from helping trauma survivors. Every time helpers interact with clients, they are putting themselves at risk. Vicarious Trauma is nothing we deserve to feel ashamed of; it is a natural stress response to the difficult work we want to do well.

This workbook is designed to follow *DAY AFTER DAY THE PRICE YOU PAY: Managing Your Second - Hand Shock*™, which is an educational resource for all people in the helping professions, or any layperson who is an active listener. We assume that you have or strongly suggest that you read *DAY AFTER DAY THE PRICE YOU PAY: Managing Your Second - Hand Shock*™ before attempting this workbook. In conjunction with the exercises you will need a journal to work with. As you proceed with this workbook, take your time and utilize this guide in a way that will best serve your individual needs.

Notes

Chapter 2: Do I Have Vicarious Trauma?

Notes

Assessing Vicarious Trauma takes some introspection and contemplation. Many of its associated symptoms are attributed to different causes, real or imagined. It will take time for you to identify and categorize them in a pattern that helps you to understand that you may be suffering from Vicarious Trauma.

At first, you may think you cannot relate to some of the following questions. However, take time to consider them and reach deep within yourself to come up with an answer. Many people are in denial about having Vicarious Trauma because so much stigma and punitive action are attached to having it. Helpers are resistant to consider the possibility that it is happening to them, so they suffer in silence. Sadly, many helpers also close off their own personal histories. They stuff them away because they are too painful to recall or to address. Yet, an awareness of one's history is absolutely necessary in the prevention and treatment of Vicarious Trauma. Instead, we choose distracting behaviors that inevitably fail us miserably. If you are working in a helping profession or if you are simply a good friend or an active listener, this set of qualifying questions may likely lead you to complete this workbook.[1]

EVALUATION QUESTIONS

Get Analytical About the Type Of Work That You Do

Sometimes we get lost in the minutia of our jobs and lose sight of the bigger picture. Take some time here to look at the nature of your work from the outside looking in.

What do you do for a living?   Counsellor

Are you in a helping capacity in your work?   Yes

---

1   Acknowledgement and thanks go to Karen Saakvitne and Laurie Anne Pearlman for their workbook, *Transforming the Pain: A Workbook on Vicarious Traumatization for Helping Professionals Who Work with Traumatized Clients.* New York: Norton, 1996.

Notes

How many hours of your week do you engage in your professional focus?

— 18

Do you work more than 25 hours directly listening to people's stories each week?

NO

Do you work with difficult clients?

yes

Do you perceive that you have choices about the people you work with?

yes

Do you have a break during the day for personal time? If so, what do you do?

No.

Do you have adequate staffing or supervision?

yes?

Who are the clients you feel most challenged with and why?

long term – deep relationship
traumatized –

Do you feel adequately trained to perform your work functions?

yes

Is your training appropriate for your work?

yes

Looking at Yourself as a Professional

Sometimes the boundary between who we are and what we do becomes blurred. Take a moment here to remember your professional identity as a part of who you are.

Do you enjoy your work? What do you like most? What do you like least?

Client work
yes

Connect
growth
seeing them
change

Lack of
team.
Some sense of
isolation

Notes

Do you see yourself as respected in your field? *Yes*

Are you financially well-compensated for your work? *Yes*

Do you feel you provide value to the clients you work with? *Yes*

Is your motivation and desire to be in your field the same as when you began this work? *I don't think so.*

Do you work in fear of making a mistake for which you will be punished? *No.*

Describe your professional style. For example, are you directive, psychoanalytical, cognitive, passive, aggressive, systems oriented? *relationship focus → Person Centred.*

Has a client ever frightened you? *No.*

What are some of the evaluations made by your clients about you that have been disturbing? *No one has said.*

Has anyone ever written you a complaint letter? What did they say? *Yes* *??* *that I did not give appropriate response —*

Has anyone ever filed a formal complaint about you to your licensing board or other authority? If so, what was the complaint? *No*

What aspects of your work concern you? *That I have enough: To listen I dislike labels... To hear + the process in organisat. To respond appears to be protecting it self? the focus self.*

135

Notes

Do you feel safe in your work? If your answer is no, in what areas do you feel at risk?

Yes

Do you have anyone to talk to about your fears at work, someone with whom you can be completely honest?

SPV unaw Chris

Looking at Yourself as a Person

This part of the workbook offers you the opportunity for introspection. This is your chance to be honest with yourself about some of the challenges you may face, just like any other human being.

Do you feel emotionally equipped to handle the distress of your clients?

most of the time

Do you have a personal trauma history?

Attachment

Has your sense of being connected to a higher order of things spirituality changed? Do you feel your spirit is broken?

I have been feeling isolated with less grounding in who I am

Has your world-view changed?

Do you recognize your strong feeling states?

Sometimes .   *NO*

Are you feeling satisfied with your family connections?

no less contact boys. Always asking if I'm doing it right

Are you suffering from any chronic or intermittent unexplained physical symptoms?

I tend to be avoidant so this is hard.

Notes

Are you sleeping well? *most of the time*

Do you worry? *yes*

Are you happy? *So - So*

Do you make time for personal enjoyment?
I think so

What do you do to relax? *Walking*
Cello - need to start swimming

Do you believe you have intimacy in your relationships?
Not sure

Do you exercise? *yes*

Do you perceive yourself as being safe in the world?
yes

EXERCISE: Act of Courage

Write down five symptoms you have identified through this assessment that you think may be symptoms of Vicarious Trauma.

1. *Not happy*
2. *Worry*
3. *chronic physical symptoms*
4. *Distance.*
5. *Overwhelmed*

EXERCISE: Act of Faith

Write down five things that would be different and better for you if you allowed yourself to heal from the reality of Vicarious Trauma:

1. Openness
2. Happiness
3. less weary
4. enjoyment in life
5. family connected — not weary

Now you have begun your journey. You have started to courageously explore and assess aspects of your work and your personal history that may contribute to your vulnerability to Vicarious Trauma. It is important that you now take this new consciousness to the next level. The reality of Vicarious Trauma is nothing to be ashamed of. It is certainly no surprise that professional helpers would fall prey to this insidious syndrome. Be accepting of your struggle and make a commitment to move forward and address this painful issue.

Notes

Chapter 3: Rapid Advance Process

Notes

Since Vicarious Trauma is experienced as a painful inner transformation in an individual's identity, it makes sense that the greatest negative impact can be described as a break in the essence or the spirit of the individual. Because helping professionals internalize trauma stories over time through the strain of controlled empathy, it should not be surprising that these helpers find themselves poor or broken in spirit. The core spiritual identity, the basic essence of the helper, becomes nearly inaccessible.

The spirit of helping individuals can be identified as that level of consciousness that rises above upset and stress and responds to negative situations with dynamics such as courage, faith, hope, trust and forgiveness. The neurocircuitry of trauma makes it very challenging to access the higher brain without a conscious and concerted effort. When people are in a state of disconnect from this powerful higher perspective, they are left with lower primitive brain reactions such as fear and anxiety as their primary context for perceiving the world. They become stuck in self-definition that is pessimistic and judgmental.

In addition, the experience of the Miracle Worker Reverie, discussed in Chapter 6 in *DAY AFTER DAY THE PRICE YOU PAY: Managing Your Second - Hand Shock*™, puts helping professionals in a position that is diametrically opposed to a healthy spiritual connection. The Reverie has helpers almost competing with their own value system, morals and ethics rather than connecting with a healthy perception of their higher self.

Vicarious Trauma leaves individuals at great risk of separation from the spiritual perspective or the higher brain. An individual's sense of spiritual identity, a very personal and individualized experience, is free from self-judgment. Vicarious Trauma puts the helper in the position of self-regard that attacks one's fundamental nature and states: "I am powerless; I am depressed." Or the opposite: "I am omnipotent; I am god-like."

Treatment must include a viable method for bridging or reconnecting to the higher mind so helpers can remain peaceful, healthy, centered, open, neutral and positive in their work. Vicarious Trauma precipitates an Impasse in the helper's *Spiritual Bridge* or neural pathway to that higher level of consciousness. Recovery from Vicarious Trauma must include some way to mend that Impasse and restore the neural pathway to the higher left brain or the spiritual point of view.

Notes

Before embarking on this journey of recovery, first clear your mind of any negative or counterproductive notions of spirituality. Many people were raised with religious dogma and practices that were either heavy handed or punitive in their orientation. Others were raised with no spiritual practice at all. Some have simply allowed that part of their experience to atrophy over time.

EXERCISE: Spirituality

Please list below any negative connotations that the word 'spirituality' elicits for you.

Dogma, restriction, wrong authority
Black & white - Dualism.
Wacky -

EXERCISE: Characters, Traits, and Behaviors

Make a list of the traits, characteristics, and behaviors you would like to create as you reconnect to your higher mind. (For example, patience, peacefulness, absence of worry, tolerance, hope, joy.)

openness, patience, joy, acceptance
stopping worrying, hope. Contemplated
A fresh relationship with the 'Other'

What would that part of you feel like?

At peace - greater sense of wholeness.

How would that part be of assistance to you when you feel troubled? Please do not rush through this segment. *I would feel held...*
grounded and more secure in who I am

You are now ready to proceed with the Rapid Advance Process. By complet-

Notes

ing the next five chapters you will have the opportunity to mend, build, and strengthen a strong neural pathway to your higher brain. In so doing, you will have the opportunity to develop a reliable practice of accessing your own remarkable internal resources for dealing with the stresses of your work and the resulting anguish or numbness of Vicarious Trauma.

The Rapid Advance model consists of five steps for Vicarious Trauma recovery:

1. Reveal the History
2. Recognize the Impasse
3. Release the Past
4. Respond to Fear
5. Reconnect with the Spirit

Please remember that this is not a substitute for treatment of recovered memories from traumatizing events earlier in one's life. This technique is for victims of Vicarious Trauma. If you are an adult survivor of serious untreated childhood trauma, we caution you about engaging in a helping profession without first receiving appropriate treatment for your psychological injuries. To do so would compromise your effectiveness and objectivity as a helping professional.

Come along with us as we take Daniel, a family lawyer, through the five steps of the Rapid Advance Process. Accompanying him on his journey will help you to focus on applying the steps for yourself. First, let us introduce you to him.

Daniel: A Case Study

Daniel was referred for treatment by his primary care physician following an annual physical. He had met with his doctor due to multiple physical annoyances. When his doctor found nothing medically wrong, he suggested that Daniel might be experiencing physical symptoms due to psychological stress and referred him to us.

Daniel presented as a man sophisticated in many dimensions. He was well-dressed, well-spoken, confident, calm and charming and really didn't understand why he was referred for a Vicarious Trauma consultation. Daniel's success as a family lawyer had its benefits and its disadvantages. While he was very conscious of all the benefits he had enjoyed from a thriving practice, he

Notes

was less conscious of how the stress in his work affected his psyche. After some interaction with him about the definition of Vicarious Trauma and after asking him the assessment questions, he experienced an "aha" moment. He was visibly concerned with how he had unwittingly been traumatized through the nature of his work.

Daniel was married for over 20 years and had 3 teenage boys. He reported he worked over 60 hours a week as a family lawyer and that he was extremely successful financially. He stated that his work took its toll on him, but that the financial rewards were worth the effort. He had provided a lavish life style for his family and wanted to keep it that way.

He shared that he was involved in a case where he was spending long hours and worrying excessively. After worrying for a couple of weeks, he started developing headaches and digestive problems. "This case is taking years off my life," he said. We asked him to elaborate. He told the tale of a client with young children seeking a divorce. This father of three wanted joint custody of his children and was working two jobs and juggling time so he could parent his kids. The wife, according to his client, was vindictive and angry because he had left the relationship, and most recently, she had made allegations that he was sexually inappropriate with the middle son. The client vehemently denied the behavior and asked Daniel to help him gain custody of the children.

Daniel related an unusually high stress level around this particular case, and stated that he felt overwhelmed when working on it at his office. He felt estranged from his family and toiled late nights and weekends just to catch up. He said his wife complained about his late hours and lack of time spent with her and the boys. He admitted he was unable to attend his children's sporting events due to his heavy court and client schedules. This, he said, he regretted more than anything. He loved his boys and his wife, but his work was too important financially to the family. There was no time for connection right now. Work came first and he didn't have much interest in anything else.

He himself was curious about his obsessive nature when it came to the facts of this one particular case. He was having unmanageable anxiety around the allegations lodged against his client. This was a case he wanted desperately to win.

Notes

Chapter 4: Rapid Advance Process - Step 1

Notes

Reveal Your History—*It Was*

You may think that your history holds no triggers or no truly upsetting events. Nonetheless, the hippocampus of your brain holds every memory you have ever experienced. While a high percentage of helping professionals are trauma survivors, there are an equal number who are not.

There is a wide range of childhood fears, all stored in the hippocampus. These historical feeling states can be triggered repetitively through listening to the trauma content of your clients. An awareness of your historical hot buttons is crucial in the maintenance of your emotional and spiritual well-being in your work.

Here is Daniel's story for Revealing the History. Hopefully, it will stimulate your thoughts about your own childhood experiences.

Daniel: Revealing the History

Daniel was born in the Midwest and was brought up by loving parents. He was the older of two children, with a sister five years younger. She looked up to her big brother as if he were her hero. Daniel stated he and his sister grew up in excellent health. He said his childhood was idyllic and that nothing was remarkable.

We first asked Daniel to describe his parents as he could remember them from a very young age. The five words he used to describe his father were passive, deferring, compliant, good provider, and absent. He related that his father was passive and deferred in most instances to his mother. If something was important to his father, he would speak up. Otherwise, he was fairly reserved. Daniel didn't bond strongly with his father, who worked many hours in order to provide financial security for the family.

> Some Common Childhood Fears
>
> A dark closet
> Being accosted by a scary child
> Being caught in the rain
> Coming home from school and having no one in the house
> Hearing strange noises
> Having nightmares
> Losing a friend
> Losing a love
> Accidents
> Feeling publicly embarrassed in school or in front of the family
> Becoming ill and missing out on important activities
> Surgery
> Hospital stays
> Shyness in school
> Moving

Notes

The five words he used to describe his mother were strong, caring, strict, perfectionistic, and nurturing. He added that his mother was extremely socially conscious and her reputation in the community was a very important part of her identity. He described his parents as affectionate and caring toward each other. If there was any conflict, it was handled behind closed doors.

Daniel described himself as an overachieving child whose primary purpose was to be an excellent reflection of his family. He excelled in school, was on the debate team, played tennis, and was accepted to an Ivy League College. He was rarely disciplined as a child since he rarely made any mistakes. Daniel was raised in the Jewish faith, attended religious education, attained his Bar Mitzvah, and celebrated high holy days and other holidays with his nuclear and extended family.

His family went through a difficult time at around age 14, when Daniel's father lost his business. Money was tight, his father was emotionally tighter, and his mother was scared. This situation resolved about a year later when Daniel's father obtained other suitable employment. During the financial crisis, he recalls his father going through the house turning off all the lights and stating, "What do you think—we own the electric company?" Daniel learned during that time to study in his room with a flashlight. He was relieved when this period was over.

The family spent quality time together going to amusement parks, the zoo, playing games together, attending theatre, movies, the children's extracurricular activities, and family dinners. He fondly recalled the home-cooked meals every night and the family discussions around the dinner table.

An emerging pattern that Daniel began to reveal was one of perfectionism and performance. The image of the family was treated as more important than identifying conflicting issues that, when confronted, usually help family members to grow. Daniel identified, after revealing his history, that he never wanted to be seen as a disappointment to his parents.

Notes

EXERCISE: History

The following questions will help build your awareness of historical feeling states or experiences that may seem like normal events to you, but may still be trigger points. You may also have significant recollections of events, but you may not have an awareness of the body memories and the visceral counterparts of these memories. Some events may have been processed and laid to rest and you may not have considered them in this context. However, revealing your history thoroughly is paramount to resolving the phenomenon of Vicarious Trauma.

As you move through the exercises below, be patient. Go slowly and become introspective in a gentle and self-accepting manner. The purpose of revealing your history is not to judge or evaluate; it is simply to honor and acknowledge.

Your Parents, Your Family, and Your Worldly Attachments

Use five adjectives to describe your early memories of your mother:

1.
2.
3.
4.
5.

Use five adjectives to describe your early memories of your father:

1.
2.
3.
4.
5.

Did your family suffer a life-altering event such as a death or divorce? If so, how was this addressed by your immediate family?

Notes

If you lived in a blended family system, please describe the dynamics associated with this experience.

Imagine watching an old movie of yourself as a child. Describe what you see.

Use five adjectives to describe your parents' marriage:

1.
2.
3.
4.
5.

How did your parents or stepparents resolve their conflicts? What did you see? What did you hear or not hear?

How did you feel when your parents or stepparents were having conflicts?

How did you feel when conflicts went unaddressed by your family?

How did your parents or stepparents handle issues around money?

How did your parents or stepparents handle issues around religion?

Notes

How did your parents or stepparents handle issues around food?

How did your family have fun together?

How was affection displayed in your family?

How were issues around sex approached in your family?

How was illness addressed in your family?

Was there any addiction or substance abuse in your family? If so, how did it you affect you?

What was the role of extended family?

How were you disciplined?

How were your relationships with your siblings? What was your birth order?

Notes

What are your most vivid memories?

What were your greatest joys as a child?

What scared you as a child?

What were some ways you used to distract yourself when you felt afraid or upset? Some examples might be daydreaming, thumb sucking, nail biting, masturbating, nightmares, bed wetting, temper tantrums, withdrawal, bullying, underachieving, overachieving, lying, or crying.

How did you get attention?

Did you have any behavioral problems as a child?

Did you have any particular challenges in growing up that stand out in your memory, such as poverty, illness, learning disabilities, disappointments, deaths, or divorce?

Your Educational Experiences

Describe your experience in elementary school.

Notes

Describe your experience in middle school.

Describe your experience in high school.

Did you change schools while you were growing up? If so, how often?

If you moved, how did it affect your relationships?

How did your parents explain the moves?

How did your family communicate about important life changes?

Describe any other significant relationships that you had while growing up: friendships, romances, relationships with grandparents, aunts, uncles, teachers or other authority figures, peer groups, extracurricular activities you participated in, and so on.

Notes

EXERCISE: Patterns from History

What patterns do you see emerging as you reveal certain aspects of your history? How you developed and evolved is important to how you cope today. Our goal here is for that to become identifiable to you. You may come up with a pattern of your own that is not mentioned here. No one knows your history better than you do!

Some Patterns You May Acknowledge
Avoidant
Passive
Aggressive
Passive-Aggressive
Abusive
Neglectful
Overprotective
Depressed
Anxious
Disconnected
Numb
Silent
Addictive
Oppositional
Bystanding
Perfectionistic

EXERCISE: Judgments and Evaluations

After revealing your history, identify and write down some judgments and evaluations you began to make about yourself and your place in the world as you moved through the early developmental stages of life. For example, children who had a chronically ill mother may have perceived themselves as abandoned and alone, as a caretaker for that parent, or as a surrogate partner for the other parent. Another example is adopted children who may have frequently felt sad because they perceived themselves as outsiders or in a state of perpetual disconnect. Children of addictive parents may have judged themselves unworthy of attention and regard because the addictive substance took over the family system. Children of divorce may have judged themselves as the cause and therefore not lovable enough to keep the family intact.

These types of self-judgments, while untrue, are natural conclusions for children to draw because, at an early stage of development, children are egocentric and tend to perceive themselves as the center of the universe. As adults, it is our wish for you to begin to identify and address these faulty core beliefs.

Write down the judgments you made about yourself as a child growing up in the context of your family.

Notes

Chapter 5: Rapid Advance Process - Step 2

Notes

Recognizing Your Impasse—*It Is*

History repeats itself. Even history that we don't recall repeats itself. Revealing your history is an empowering first step. Now we would like you to consider how you might unwittingly re-create some early patterns in your current life that you have already identified in the preceding chapter.

Those who have unconscious or unresolved fears and judgments about themselves are at risk of repeating the pattern in their primary relationships, in their parenting, and in their work. They are also at the greatest risk for suffering unidentified Vicarious Trauma.

The Impasse is defined as an emotional and physiological fear reaction, that point of a fear reaction that has its roots in our history. This reaction has three dimensions: 1) the memory itself, 2) the negative feeling you have attached to it, and 3) the judgment we make of ourselves and the others involved in it. When triggered, we continue to distract ourselves, believing that it is a form of self-protection, when in reality the only thing that is being protected is the historical fear itself. The unconscious purpose of defending your Impasse is to protect yourself from ever having to feel the fear that originated in early childhood. Children normally find ways to distract themselves from feeling afraid simply because fear is an overwhelming feeling state. A child does not yet possess the skills or the internal tools to manage fear.

As adults, rather than resort to distraction from the fear, we need to recognize it, turn into it, and overcome it. Until now, we have used various distractions to avoid the unpleasant feeling state. Our goal now is to no longer distract ourselves. Distraction is historically based, and we deserve and need to recognize the distraction we are unconsciously using to cover the original fear that drove the historically based distraction. We are now ready to move into the fear and not into the distraction. Let us recognize the originating fear and identify it. We will call this the Impasse.

Here is Daniel's experience with this step.

Daniel: Recognizing the Impasse

Our job now was to help Daniel discover, in what was a seemingly innocuous family history, the emotional Impasse that was being triggered for him

Notes

through this particular case. When the client in question came to retain Daniel and proceeded to talk about the alleged sexual impropriety, Daniel noticed himself feeling agitated and anxious. He would come to understand that he was at an Impasse and he was compromised in his ability to remain professionally present.

When asked to recall an event in growing up that really stood out for him, he paused and then began to share with us a rather enlightening historical event. When he was 6 years old, he and a group of neighborhood children were playing in a neighbor's garage. They were playing doctor, examining each other and looking at the differences in their anatomy. The little girls were fascinated with the fact that he had a penis and he was fascinated with their vaginas. They played for awhile and then all went home, except for him and a friend, who went to play at the friend's home. After what he recalls as about an hour, his mother called and requested that he come home immediately. Daniel left and walked home.

When he arrived, his mother and father were in the kitchen, and asked him if he had taken his pants off with the other neighborhood children. He immediately sensed that his parents were angry and he did not understand why. He innocently agreed that he did, in fact, undress and that Lori, the little girl next door, showed him her vagina and he showed her his penis.

His mother became enraged and told him to drop his pants. She was going to spank him for his behavior. She screamed at him, telling him that he embarrassed her and his dad with Lori's parents and all the other parents in the neighborhood. They contended that he did something terribly wrong and that he should never ever do it again.

He was spanked with a wooden spoon by his mother until he screamed at her to stop. During this act of corporal punishment, his father sat in the other room, silent. The subject was never again brought up in the family, as if it never happened. At this point, Daniel stated, "Wow! That's really a disturbing memory. I haven't thought of that in over 25 years." He recognized that this self-described distressing event had in fact deeply affected him. As a result of the case he was presently working on, Daniel realized that this event or Impasse carried a lot more significance for him than he was ever conscious about.

Notes

Daniel then told us that he had many friendships and relationships as his childhood progressed, but always felt uncomfortable about his body and about his sexual ability. Later, in his junior year of high school, he became serious about a girl and they began having a sexual relationship. One evening, about 6 months into the relationship, his girlfriend's father called his mother to let her know that Daniel was having sexual relations with their daughter and that they (her parents) were upset. Daniel's mother spoke with him about this conversation and directed him to discontinue his relationship with this young woman. She maintained that risking his future on a girl at this point might ruin his chances for college and law school. He related that, several days later, in silent resentment and grief, he broke up with his girlfriend. He did this to avoid disappointing his mother and to avoid a conflict. He could now see that this was one of numerous other times he had unwittingly re-created his original Impasse.

After Daniel told us his story, we asked him if he felt these incidents broke his spirit. His facial expression visibly softened and he sank back into his chair. He said, "You're so right. I never thought of it that way," and he began to weep.

The self-protective distractions of our childhood mature as we develop. Now that you have revealed your history, you are able to become conscious about and recognize how you find yourself at your own Impasse repeatedly in adulthood and even more so through your work as a helper.

EXERCISE: Childhood Distractions and Coping Mechanisms

Let us recognize how this applies to you. Think again and repeat the identification of childhood distractions/coping mechanisms you utilized when you felt afraid. List them below.

Notes

EXERCISE: Evolved Distractions

Now contemplate the more adult behaviors that you do today that might be considered "evolved distractions" of your childhood reactions to fear. For example; a thumb sucker or a nail biter may now be a cigarette smoker; a shy child may be a socially withdrawn adult; a child that used illness for attention may be chronically ill as an adult, an overachiever may turn into a workaholic,;and a bully might grow up to struggle with road rage. List the adult distractions you use below.

When you peel away the distractions, you might notice that you are experiencing anxiety. Underlying historical fear is an internally divisive dynamic, a primitive, lower brain neurocircuitry that inhibits individuals from accessing their higher mind. As a child, you hadn't yet fully formed your pre-frontal cortex. This area of the brain embodies the higher mind and the behavioral responses of courage, trust, and faith in one's ability to overcome fear. (See Chapter 2, The Neuroscience of Trauma, *Day After Day The Price You Pay: Managing Your Second - Hand Shock*™, 2008.) The anxiety people feel when they stop distracting themselves is a form of separation anxiety, emptiness, or void, resulting from being in disconnect from the higher mind.

As an adult, this part of your brain has developed and needs to be more regularly accessed as a healthy coping mechanism for dealing with trauma. Training our brains to move into this higher functioning is derailed when we continue to distract it with childhood coping mechanisms rather than adult responses. Our goal is to mend the spiritual bridge or neural pathway to your spiritual mind and that part of your higher brain.

Notes

EXERCISE: Journaling

A. It is now time to think about and write down some client stories that you have felt particularly uncomfortable with or that evoked a body reaction—like anger or anxiety—after listening to the content. Use your journal for this exercise.

B. Recognize when you are playing an updated version of an historical scene and allow yourself to experience rather than avoid the unpleasant separation anxiety that gets triggered in the replay. You need to experience your legitimate anxiety in order to heal.

C. Now write in your journal a personal historical story that comes to mind for you by virtue of having listened to the client's narrative.

After you have finished journaling, say to yourself, "Something is getting triggered in me. This is not about the client. This is about what the client's story is activating in my own historical neurocircuitry. It's okay that this is going on for me. I will not judge it. I will remain calm so that I may identify what is coming to the surface. By identifying and getting conscious of it, I will better serve my client. Also, I don't have to react the way I did as a child. I am an adult now and have other choices. I do not have to distract myself from this upset in order to prevail. Instead, I need to feel it, move through it, and remember that my incident was in the past and does not have to hold any meaning for me in the present. It is powerless over me today."

D. Write down the subjects that trigger your Impasses. Some examples might be childhood violence, molestation, abandonment, corporal punishment, divorce, death of a family member, death of a child, moving, an angry father or mother, a passive mother or father, peer rejection, failure at something you attempted, bullying, cheating, accidents, foul weather, illness, addictions, neglect, certain words, the parental "look," and so on.

E. Put your Impasse into words in your journal. Remember, your Impasse contains your memory of the event, your feeling about the event when it happened, and how you judged yourself or others involved in light of the event.

Notes

No one knows your Impasse better than you. Develop an inner awareness of your Impasse and make friends with it. Don't avoid it any more. Right now, we ask you to recognize it so you can move forward and think peacefully about it.

Notes

Chapter 6: Rapid Advance Process - Step 3

Notes

Your unconscious attachment to some parts of your past prohibit you from bridging to the higher mind or spiritual self, which is the most powerful and peaceful part of you. The spiritual self stays peacefully centered in the here and now. Having identified your Impasse and deciding to no longer retreat from it, you can begin to mend the break in your spiritual bridge. It is important to note that this break widens in your work with trauma content. By releasing the past, you can exchange your purpose from protecting an historical fear, to healing your connection to hope and peacefulness. You are now beginning to form more remedial neural pathways that will empower you to negotiate trauma material more resourcefully.

In releasing the past you must remember that your memories don't equal the past. What you remember has far less impact than how you remember it. The historical action itself is over. It is only your judgment of yourself and others in its context that remains. For example, if you have a memory of being disciplined by an aggressive parent, there may be a childlike part of you that remembers this event with embarrassment or shame, believing in some way that you were not worthy of receiving love. The memory itself is far less damaging than your perception of who you are in light of it. If you are working with a client who is grieving about abuse suffered at the heavy hand of a parent or spouse, you yourself may go into a shame spiral due to the triggering of your own childhood Impasses.

You can heal your perception of a painful historical event anytime you choose to relinquish judgment of that event. Let's witness how Daniel addressed his own historical judgments.

Daniel: Releasing the Past

As Daniel acknowledged and honored his Impasse, he realized that the boy who was spanked perceived himself as dirty, inappropriate and not deserving of being loved. His memory of playing doctor with the neighborhood children was not as troublesome as his judgment of himself around it, which was that he was an inappropriate child who deserved to be punished. How sad for little Daniel, we pointed out, for he was only having normal childhood curiosity about the human anatomy.

Notes

Daniel worked to release his past by relinquishing judgment around the spanking. He realized for the first time that much of the shame he carried actually belonged to his mother, who herself was embarrassed within her community by her son's participation in playing doctor. Her son should have known better.

As a young boy in that event, Daniel judged his mother as perpetrating, attacking, rejecting, and angry. He judged his father as abandoning, powerless, and absent. As an adult, Daniel has the choice to no longer attribute these judgments to himself, his mother, or his father. He exchanged his purpose from fear to forgiveness and in so doing released his painful perception of that aspect of his past.

EXERCISE: Impasse Memories

A. Review the historical events that you identified as Impasses.

B. Associate the feelings you had with those particular Impasse memories. (Painful memories might typically elicit feeling states of sadness, embarrassment, shame, disappointment, anger, or fear. These feelings, untreated, may generate a personal and professional sense of inadequacy. Daniel put the following feelings around his Impasse: shame, sadness, anger, and, most of all, fear of disappointing his parents.)

C. List the judgments you've made about yourself or others around these Impasse events.

Notes

EXERCISE: Exchanging Fear for Forgiveness

In order to relinquish the judgment, you need to exchange your fear for forgiveness.

A. Admit you have the fear. Write down what you are afraid of. (For example, I have a fear of not being good enough, of being stupid, embarrassed.)

B. Take personal responsibility for the role your memory is playing in your life and decide what it is you want to create around this memory.

C. Realize the judgment you have placed on the event and on the person or persons in the event with you. List these judgments.

Something I May Want to Create a Memory Around
healing
peace
calmness
closure
release or forgiveness versus resentment
anger
hostility
grievance
continued pain
vengeance
depression
anxiety or physical illness

D. Remove all descriptors (adjectives or adverbs) that depict the event.

> Daniel did this by writing in his journal:
> "I was playing doctor with my friends and we were curious about each other's bodies and examined each other. We were different, as some of us were girls and some were boys. I took my pants off and the girl next door took her pants off. We giggled because I had a penis and she didn't. That was it, nothing more. We pulled up our pants and went out to play. Later that night my mother asked me if I took off my clothes at Lori's house. I said yes. She hit me with a wooden spoon on my bare bottom until I cried. It just was—it's not happening now and I don't need to feel anything about it at all. I certainly don't need to be afraid. If my mother came at me with a wooden spoon today, I could protect myself and stop her. As a child, I had no recourse. My parents' past

Notes

disapproval doesn't mean I am a bad child. I am choosing to release this feeling of unworthiness because I can."

E.   Remove all your judgments, unconsciously made at an earlier time, from the description of the event. Commit to exchanging your fear around this event with forgiveness: forgiveness of yourself and forgiveness of the others who were involved. You do not have to forgive the event itself. The event may not have been okay. You are forgiving yourself and the other people involved so you can be released. Remember, this forgiveness is not for them—it is for you to be free. It is through your forgiveness of the other person that you can be released from a painful past.

F.   Write in your journal, I forgive...........(for example, my mother for hitting me with a wooden spoon, and I forgive myself for)...................(for example, any negative self-judgments I have made in light of or because of this event).

Forgiveness is for people, not for actions. Spanking is an action; the fact that you were spanked doesn't mean you were bad. Maybe you engaged in behavior that was unacceptable; that doesn't mean you are unacceptable. You made a mistake, you are not a mistake.

EXERCISE: Personal Obstacles

What are your personal obstacles to forgiveness (for example, some people see themselves as justified in bearing grievances)?

In deciding to release the past, you can move from fear to forgiveness. Forgiveness is the relinquishment of judgment followed by a thought of peace. You can now remember that in light of a painful memory, you remain worthy of compassion and regard. The thoughts of peace will serve you in your next step: responding to fear.

Notes

Chapter 7: Rapid Advance Process - Step 4

Notes

Respond To Your Fear—I Know

There is a big difference between responding and reacting. Reacting involves little or no spiritual connection. It is based on the primitive brain's instinct of fight or flight and is defensive in nature. We react when we perceive the need to protect ourselves. If we take ourselves back to the first step, we are invested in protecting ourselves from feeling historical fears. To do so is faulty thinking and a dangerous place to put yourself in the helping relationship.

Responding involves the introduction of a reply or an answer and is associated with the conscious left brain. Take a second and consider how you tend to answer in emotionally charged or fearful conditions. Daniel, the family lawyer in our case study, would become a perfectionist and a workaholic when he felt afraid.

Once we have relinquished our earlier self-judgment that was unconsciously made, we need to stay peaceful when we are presented with an upsetting work situation that triggers fear from our primitive brain. Responding, rather than reacting, implies thinking peacefully or calmly when we are deciding what to do or what to say in a fear-provoking situation. Responding rather than reacting to emotional fear is the most important part of recovering from Vicarious Trauma. Responding is a discipline. It requires a great deal of mental structure and practice in order to become proficient.

Now that you have revealed your history, recognized your Impasse, and made a commitment to release the past, you are ready to respond to the historical fear that is triggered through your personal relationships and your work.

EXERCISE: Stop, Look, and Listen

Do you remember this phrase being taught to you as a child when you were learning to cross the street? Some streets are easier to cross than others. At some of the dangerous intersections, you could easily be mowed down by a vehicle if you didn't adhere to the rule. When you find yourself at a scary emotional intersection in your work, the rule of responding is to stop, look, and listen.

Stop: Identify what will become your personal red light. What was once a burden in your distraction from fear can now serve as a blessing that signals

Notes

that something is being triggered for you. Simply stop. What is your adult distraction when you feel afraid? Here are some possibilities: raging, numbing out, drinking, drugs, withdrawing, isolating, stealing, shopping, dissociating, impatience, passivity, eating disorders, working too much, headaches, stomachaches, ringing in the ears, intrusive thoughts, nightmares, sleeping, fuzzy thinking, and forgetting to breathe. What are yours? Keep in mind that it could be more than one symptom.

Possible Adult Distractions
Raging
Numbing out
Drinking
Drugs
Withdrawing
Isolating
Stealing
Shopping
Dissociating
Impatience
Passivity
Eating disorders
Working too much
Headaches
Stomach aches
Ringing in the ears
Intrusive thoughts
Nightmares
Sleeping
Fuzzy thinking
Forgetting to breathe

Look: Look inside, become introspective, and think about what is being triggered in your history. Acknowledge it. Honor it. Relinquish judgment about yourself and others involved. Think peacefully about it. Forgive it. For example, if your paternal abandonment is being triggered by a client's story, and you have stopped the distracting behaviors you used to engage in, you have freed yourself to look inward and reveal your truth about what is happening.

Listen: Listen to your inner voice and your inner truth.

EXERCISE: Journaling

A. Go to your journal and write about a time when a particular client story triggered something personal for you. As you write it, listen peacefully to your inner story and realize that you deserve to forgive, to be forgiven, and to be more patient with yourself and the traumatizing aspects of your work.

B. Write your story so that the concluding line is "May this story rest in peace."

Notes

Practice the two forgiveness steps:
1) relinquishing judgment, followed by
2) thoughts of peace.

C. In the space below, make a forgiveness list for hurts you have incurred in your personal life and in the workplace. Every story is an opportunity for practicing forgiveness, which has been coined for centuries as being divine.

D. Make a list of all the people you want to forgive and include the things for which you believe you need to be forgiven.

This practice is universally healing, and those doing the forgiving are successfully bridging to their higher mind, creating new-found hope, faith, and meaning in their life, and, ultimately, in their work.

Let's have a look at how our client Daniel responded to fear.

Daniel: Responding to Fear

As he recognized the Impasse and relinquished the self-judgment, Daniel became aware of when the historical fear of being unworthy and a disappointment was triggered in his work and in his family. He could now respond to this fear rather than distract himself from it by working harder, obsessing about a particular case, or becoming physically ill. He began to practice thinking peacefully about that painful childhood event, forgiving his parents and himself. He was able to notice more frequently when he was triggered in his work. When he became perfectionistic, he stopped, looked within and listened to his inner story. Instead of being traumatized vicariously, he remembered what was really going on for him and responded to the fear with kindness

and peace unto himself. By doing this repeatedly, he began to mend the break in his spiritual bridge and develop an improved neural pathway to his higher brain, which he could now more easily access.

Notes

Chapter 8: Rapid Advance Process - Step 5

Notes

Reconnect To Your Spirit—*I Am*

This is the most rewarding part of the process. There is nothing you have to do. There is nothing you have to figure out. Simply let your mind be still. Now that you are no longer distracted, anxious, worried, or fearful, you have opened the way to clear your mind and allow your neurons to bridge to your higher mind, in which you receive the characteristics or traits of higher mind thinking.

Now that you are no longer distracted and can let your mind be still, you are empowered to start engaging in some practice that will allow wisdom, calm and peaceful thoughts into your experience. Let your mind receive and connect to them. Develop a spirituality/peace plan, something that you do daily, weekly or monthly to clear your mind and allow spiritual traits to come into your thinking.

Possible Spirituality/Peace Plan
Meditation
Prayer
Nature hikes
Gardening
12-step programs
Connecting with others
Speaking your truth
Engaging in the arts
Reading
Journaling
Playing games
Expressing gratitude
Exercising
Joining an encouragement group
Dancing
Cooking

EXERCISE: Wish List

Write down all the things that you wish you had time to do and haven't been able to fit into your schedule.

EXERCISE: Modifying Your Schedule

Look at your schedule and see how you can modify it so that your personal spirit has time to rejuvenate. Put in blocks of time throughout your schedule to release the pressures and stresses of the day and see where you can fit in some of the things you have wanted to do but have not prioritized.

Notes

EXERCISE: Affirmations

Make five affirmations that you can repeat—one for each day of the work week. For example:

- I am going to face my week with courage, tolerance and patience.
- My work is busy and meaningful. I am grateful for the help I can give.
- I will be introspective today. I will think of any upsetting situations that have occurred so far and address them with the techniques I have learned.
- Today I will nurture myself—the work week is drawing to a close and I will plan some self-fulfilling activities in the two or three days ahead.
- I have completed a challenging week. There have been satisfying and taxing experiences. I have helped others and learned some important things about myself.
- I have stayed in the present and not allowed my past to dictate how I lead my life today.
- I have not been distracted with inappropriate behaviors—I am proud of my recovery from Vicarious Trauma and will continue to work on it every day.

Now, write your own.
1.
2.
3.
4.
5.

Commit to following through with your plan.

Here is a final look at Daniel as he reconnected to his higher mind.

Daniel: Reconnecting to the Spirit

Daniel saw us for five sessions. During the fifth session he reported that since he was thinking more peacefully, he noticed a renewed ability to utilize abstract spiritual behaviors such as hope, courage and faith in himself. He relaxed more around his cases, set clearer boundaries in his work life, and spent more time with his family. As Daniel became more conscious of remembering his spiritual connection, he was able to pick and choose from

Notes

his own religious historical practices things he could draw upon, add to and share with his family. He terminated his treatment with us feeling a rich gratitude for all the wonderful things in his life: his personal well-being, a loving wife, great kids, and a rewarding career.

This is a creative journey. You will decide how to build a spiritual perspective that fits into your lifestyle and belief system. Any combination of behaviors that fit for you will work—it's a very personal creation. Communing with nature, sitting in a sauna, relaxing in a hammock, reading a book, spending time with loved ones, gardening, cooking, singing, getting a massage, exercising, whatever brings you joy. It doesn't have to be religious in nature, although it could be. Or it could be a patchwork design representing a number of gratifying activities. Whatever resonates for you.

We wish you peace.

Notes

Chapter 9: Conclusion - Spread the Word!

Notes

It is our hope that completing this workbook has given you appreciation and new-found sensitivity to the stressors of your work. We hope this has struck a cord in you that will allow you to become passionate about the reality of Vicarious Trauma and spread the word in your helping circles and around your community in general. We encourage you to consider starting Vicarious Trauma support groups and/or staff meetings where traumatizing interactions can be debriefed and resolved.

We aspire to raise the social consciousness about the prevalence and seriousness of Vicarious Trauma so that helpers will be treated as precious human beings with feelings and struggles of their own. Social acknowledgement, treatment centers, recuperative programs, and retreats should be commonplace and highly available to professionals who function as helpers. We need your help in this endeavor.

Contact Information

Ellie and Vicki serve as directors of the Vicarious Trauma Institute in Scottsdale, Arizona. They can be contacted at (480) 991-4119, or by email at:

Ellie Izzo	info@vicarioustrauma.com
Vicki Carpel Miller	info@vicarioustrauma.com

The Vicarious Trauma Institute in Scottsdale, Arizona, serves clients from any and all helping professions, providing individual consultations, one to three-day intensive treatment programs and recuperative retreats. We support you in searching out any professional who is knowledgeable in this field and encourage you to utilize any resources that help address your Vicarious Trauma. We look forward to working with you.

Ellie and Vicki

Bibliography

Begley, S. (2007). Train your mind, change your brain. New York: Ballantine.

Carll, E. (2006). Trauma psychology: The evolution of a specialty. Retrieved February 28, 2007, from the APA website: http://www.division42.org

Earley, J. (2006). Transference and countertransference. Retrieved June 8, 2007, from http://www.earley.org./Patterns/transference_and_countertransfer. htm

Figley, C. R. (Ed.). (1995). Compassion fatigue: Coping with secondary traumatic stress disorder in those who treat the traumatized. New York: Brunner Mazel.

Fox, R., & Carey, L. (1999, Summer). Therapists' collusion with the resistance of rape survivors. Clinical Social Work Journal, 185-201.

Frankl, Victor. (1954). Man's search for meaning: An introduction to logotherapy. New York: Washington Square Press.

International Trauma Consultants. (2006). Retrieved March 6, 2007, from *http://www.traumaconsultants.net*

Izzo, Ellie (2007). *The bridge to I am.* New York: iUniverse

Jaffe, J., Segal, J., & Dumke, L. (2005). Emotional and psychological trauma. Retrieved February 2, 2007, from http://www.helpguide.org

Joseph, R. (1999, August 23). The neurology of traumatic 'dissociative' amnesia: Commentary and literature review. Child Abuse and Neglect, 8, 715-727.

Kramer, P. (2007). Empathy: The infinite mind. Retrieved (needs date), from http://www.kmedia.com

Kennedy, E. & Charles, S. On becoming a counselor: A basic guide for nonprofessional counselors. New York: Crossroads.

Lee, David. (2006). The hidden costs of trauma in the workplace. Retrieved March 6, 2007, from http://www.humannatureatwork.com/workplacestress

Liberzon, I., Taylor, S., Amdur, R., Jung, T., Chamberlin, K, Minoshima, S. et al. (1999). Brain activation in PTSD in response to trauma related stimuli. Biological Psychiatry, 45(7), 817-826.

Pearlman, L., & MacIan, P. (1995). An empirical study of the effects of trauma on work with trauma therapists. Professional Psychology: Research and Practice, 26(6), 558-565.

Pearlman, L., & Saakvitne, K. (1995). Treating therapists and vicarious traumatization and secondary traumatic stress disorders. In C. R. Figley (Ed.), Compassion fatigue: Coping with secondary traumatic stress disorder in those who treat the traumatized (Psychosocial Stress Series) (pp. 150-177). New York: Brunner Mazel.

Saakvitne, K., & Pearlman, L. (1996). Transforming the pain: A workbook on Vicarious Trauma. New York: Norton.

Schore, A. (2003). Advances in neuropsychoanalysis attachment theory and trauma research. Psychoanalytic Inquiry, 22, 433-484.

Stamm, B. H. (Ed.). (1995). Secondary traumatic stress: Self-care issues for clinicians,
researchers and educators. Lutherville, MD: Sidran.

Weingarten, K. (2003). Common shock. Witnessing violence every day: How we are harmed, how we can heal. New York: Dutton.

Weingarten, K. (2004, February). Common shock: Witnessing violence in clients' lives [Adaptation]. Counselor Magazine, 70-74.

Wilson, J., & Lindy, J. (1994). Countertransference in the treatment of PTSD. New York: Guilford Press.

Wilson, J., & Thomas, R. (2004). Empathy and the treatment of trauma and PTSD. New York: Brunner Mazel.

Printed in the United Kingdom by
Lightning Source UK Ltd., Milton Keynes
140485UK00001B/263/P

9 780981 509006